There is Humour in Adversity.

Ramblings of my life in Zimbabwe.

Chris Pocock

There is Humour in Adversity

ISBN:1508994781
ISBN-13:9781508994787

DEDICATION

To my family to whom this book is intended.

There is Humour in Adversity

CONTENTS

1	Melsetter	Pg	1
2	Umtali	Pg	20
3	Police	Pg	29
4	UDI and National Service	Pg	34
5	Salisbury	Pg	41
6	Que Que	Pg	46
7	Greys Scouts	Pg	57
8	Horseshoe	Pg	70
9	Horses	Pg	77
10	House Attack	Pg	90
11	Cease Fire	Pg	107
12	Family	Pg	117
13	Timber Concession	Pg	143
14	Centenery, Featherston	Pg	156
15	Safari Craft	Pg	172
16	Inflation Days	Pg	179
17	Mozambique	Pg	189
18	Finale	Pg	202

There is Humour in Adversity

AUTHOR'S NOTE

My Daughter Tara had asked me on a number of occasions to write my story for the family, she of course having lived with me through a large part of it.

I found it difficult to simply write about my life but after a number of friends persuaded me, I decided to high light the different phases we Zimbabweans have lived through during my life span and the only person's life I know really well to do this is my own.

I hope I have made this book interesting, easy to read and light hearted.

My thanks go to my sister Celia Coleman who has spent hours editing this book and as always, given me so much encouragement and to my daughter Tara for formatting the cover.

There is Humour in Adversity

CHAPTER ONE
MELSETTER

Tickey, Sixpence, Shilling and Murungupenny [white man's penny] were names the Africans liked to use in the days of the 1950's. From the time of the early settlers, it was fashionable for Africans to use European names and generally was selected at the time of birth. Names like Takesure, Tenboy, Beauty, Patience and so on, usually depicted their thought pattern at the time of birth of their child.

This was the period I grew up in the Eastern Districts of Rhodesia in a small Village known as Melsetter and to these primitive but gentle folk I learnt to speak their language of Ndou.

Melsetter lies in a basin formed by the Sky Line ridge in the west and the magnificent range of the Chimanimani Mountains in the east that borders the Portuguese held territory of Mozambique.

The Chimanimani mountain range is a breathtaking curtain of granite rock reaching high into the heavens and absorbing all the colours the rich sky has to offer. It is a favorite tourist destination and home to the 'Outward Bound' recreational facility for mountain climbers and boot camps.

Within the basin are undulating hills, some of them small and some large that feed abundant crystal clear streams of water that seep from the lush green vegetation around and within this basin lies the small village of Melsetter comprising a few shops, a garage, a Junior School, government buildings and a two story hotel with a grand view of the Chimanimani range.

The Village provided the needs of a community of fruit farmers and estates of timber plantations of Pine and Wattle trees. Today, the small farmer no longer exists having been bought out by the big estate companies and the area is now home to vast acres of pine forests with sawmills nestled in amongst it.

Cecil John Rhodes, the founder of Rhodesia, allowed a bunch of Afrikaans farmers from the Free State in South Africa to settle the Eastern Districts to secure the land that was in dispute with the Portuguese.

The Trek comprised a number of family units led by Thomas Moodie. Some broke ranks on route to settle in Fort Victoria, whilst the rest crossed the Sabi River and climbed the escarpment to what is today known as Chipingi.

The escarpment itself proved a formidable task to conquer; having to couple up three spans of oxen to haul each wagon up the incline and even some of the more well endowed ladies required a helping push from behind.

On reaching the top they gathered a pile of rocks and laid them as a memorial to their safe arrival. They called this the Ebenezer from the bible and agreed to meet on the anniversary of every five years.

Thomas Moodie decided to call this new settlement Melsetter after his ancestral home where his grandfather was the last Laird of Melsetter in the Orkney Islands, Scotland. Moodie died within the year and is buried on his farm 'Waterfall' at the top of the escarpment.

Two years later, 1894, Marthinhus Martin decided to move the settlement to the current position of Melsetter. He took the trek down into the Risitu valley and following the Nyhodi River upstream he settled the area that he now named Melsetter.

The original settlement then became known as Chipinga which is derived from the name of the local Chief Chipingi.

Martin then collected the rocks of the Ebenezer from the original site and brought them to the new Melsetter where they built a memorial out of granite that had a statue of a wagon on top and plaques of the members of each trek mounted on the sides. Within the panels these Ebenezer rocks were laid. The village was then laid out around this monument that formed the Village Square.

Our farm, 'Nyhodi' was up one side of the Nyhodi valley, parts of it steep and Dad grew Wattle for the nearby Silver Streams factory that turned the bark into tannin for processing leather.

Our home, a thatched house, was half way up the hill and commanded a magnificent view of the valley below giving my parents pre warning of any visitors arriving. It was a home I cherished and gave all three of us kids memories that we all look back on.

My brother Digby was ten years older than me and consequently was as good as another generation away. Celia my sister was eight years my senior but I had more time with her than I did Digby. She liked to dress me up as her doll, kitting me out in frilly dresses and high heel shoes that probably gave me the background for my roles as women in pantomimes many years later.

This was a place for a kid like myself to grow up, and with all the freedom in the world was able to exploit all manners of mischief to mould my formative years. Together with Gideon my friend and son of Murungupenny, I learnt to drive the

Ferguson Tractor without permission, antagonize Chimani Phoebus the aggressive Jersey bull, raise embarrassed looking chickens that had no neck feathers and grow mealies amongst Guava trees that the Africans helped indigenize by sowing the seeds with their stools whenever they went to the toilet in the bush.

I had a bantam rooster that I reared from a chick and named him 'Jongwe'. He grew into a wonderful pet and not bad looking either.

I would help my father whenever he had to repair anything and on this occasion, as his spanner boy, we were underneath the Land Rover repairing something when this inquisitive Jongwe came to peer at dads face as he lay on his back under the vehicle.

This annoyed dad intensely and Jongwe would come flying out of there followed by a spanner in hot pursuit.

Everything was a game for Jongwe and he had found a new one to antagonize dad that he seemed to relish doing.

Now he found another game. Dad would have his lunch time siesta in which we kids had to be quiet under pain of death.

Jongwe discovered if he sneaked around the veranda and entered my parents bedroom then crowed loudly, he would get a response and a response he got.

Jongwe would come bounding out of the open French doors in a mocking cackle of laughter followed by a shoe that seldom hit the mark. This was all too much for Dad and he offered me ten shillings to cut his head off.

Now ten shillings is a lot of money to a young kid and was certainly big enough to induce me to follow through on the act.

Having done it I was now mortified that this was the end of Jongwe and ten shillings paled into insignificance.

Mum ran a store at the entrance of the farm that became known as 'Peacock Store' and to this day survives under this name.

I would go behind the counter and sneak off a packet that had four different coloured chewing gums and sometimes a packet of eight Star Cigarettes.

Gideon and Solomon, his brother, and I would puff on these without inhaling. The chewing gum would remove the smell later. I would also remove all the tobacco from my parent's cigarette butts and fill empty Star boxes of this tobacco and sell it to Murungupenny and Tickey who would make 'roll your own' cigarettes using the local newspaper .

These were the days of series 1 Land Rovers, dirt

roads and mud chains chinking away on the wheels. Of a sleepy Village that had a bottle store that sold Liquorice Allsorts, a general dealers store that my first watch was procured and returned within 5 minutes because my cousin Griselda borrowed the money from my mother that was supposed to be for her own use, a hotel that the visiting Government Dentist used to tortured us with his contraption of arms and belt driven gadgets and a Junior Boarding School that I nagged to go too but no amount of dress pulling or sobbing tears would convince my mother that it was a mistake to leave me there.

Digger Ashworth was my buddy at the time. They lived further down the Nyhodi Valley on Lavinas Rust and I would spend a lot of time there particularly when my parents were on call up.

He had two very good looking sisters and often we would swim in the earth dam just below their house. On this occasion, swimming in the muddy brown water, the girls invited us to take our clothes off as they were swimming in the nude. To prove it, they stuck their white butts out of the water. Taking up the challenge we swam to the shore and removed our costumes and dived back to join them.

Unknown to us the girls had their costumes with them which they surreptitiously put on and swam back to shore and grabbing our costumes disappeared with them leaving us stranded in the dam. Never trust a woman they say and they seem to learn this at an early age.

I recall on one occasion being allowed to take the tractor and trailer with the house maids to collect a load of firewood from the top wattle plantation.

I had my friend Butch Sutton from school with me and we parked the tractor on the hill for a run start whilst the maids loaded the trailer. With Butch sitting on the mudguard of the tractor, I engaged 4th gear and rolled down the steep hill to start the engine as it had no starter and having done that, put it in neutral and applied the brakes to slow it down to engage 1st gear.

But being about nine years old I was not big or strong enough to apply the brakes and we went bouncing down the road picking up speed as we went.

Finally stopping at the bottom of the hill I looked around to check on the maids but they were not on the trailer, they had fallen off and were now limping down the road. Very disgruntled, they refused to get back on preferring to walk the rest of the way. I did get them to promise not to tell dad.

Dad had bought Nyhodi purely to be a forester growing Wattle. Wattle is a species of Acacia having the customary yellow flower and grows into a tall tree that the trunk produces a very good pole for construction. The bark is stripped off fresh and cut in lengths of four feet, bundled and sent to the factory where it is milled and boiled into a toffee like substance for tanning leather.

The Wattle Company that owned the Silver Streams processing factory, contracted out growers, of which Dad was one, to meet the volumes the factory required.

But as their own plantations came on line to meet demand, the out growers were dropped and Dad became a victim to this. Dad then turned to peaches, tomatoes and other vegetables that we kids would have fun helping Mum in the packing shed and in which she would reprimand us for eating more than we packed.

But this too proved un lucrative as the market in Salisbury was just too far away for the Road Motor Services [R.M.S.] to get it there fresh and on time. So dad turned to cattle.

The Cold Storage Commission offered a facility to farmers by providing cows that a farmer could breed from and establish his own herd.

It was a brilliant scheme that required the farmer to simply return the original herd or their replacement when he was done with them. Through this scheme, dad bought a herd of about one hundred head in Umtali and Tickey and Murungupenny walked them to the farm that took some days.

Mum went to meet them when they arrived at the Sky Line pass that is the gateway to Melsetter and Ticky reported that a heifer was footsore and unable to continue.

Mum was a city girl, always well dressed and because of her lack of height, wore high heel shoes. Undaunted, she now instructed them to load the heifer into the back of her Van Guard Station Wagon.

All was well until the heifer decided to stand up and losing its balance, fell over the back seat wedging itself upside down between the front and back seats and proceeded to bellow.

Mum pulled over and in her high heel shoes stepped onto the road and flagged down the first car that came along.

It happened to be a travelling salesman and his driver returning to Umtali from Melsetter. "Please help me, I have a cow upside down on the back seat of my car" she said with all the charm she could muster.

What went through the salesman's head at that moment can just be imagined but he and the driver were able to right the cow and send this tiny but crazy woman on her way.

And she was crazy. Blaming my father for bringing her out to this 'god forsaken land' she refused to change a wheel if she had a puncture. She would simply drive home, leaving a trail of broken rubber and dad would spend hour's panel beating buckled rims. But despite it all, Mum was a forceful character and took on everything that came her way with humour and energy.

Once a month, we would drive into Umtali along the old strip roads in the Land Rover pickup to do the grocery shopping.

I would sit in the middle with the gear stick between my legs and look forward to the tea break at the 'Tea Junction' just after the Umvumvumvu bridge where the road branches off to Birchinof Bridge on the Sabi River. They served the greatest cream scones and cook sisters and I would be allowed a milk shake.

Mum always had to look her best and before arriving, would haul out her hand bag and start giving her face a makeover. First it would be the powder puff, liberally slapped on her face and creating clouds of dust that for me, not sitting near any window, was asphyxiating. Then, after the rouge, the lip stick.

With the rear view mirror swung into focus, she would apply this lipstick to puckered lips that would take the shape of a chicken's ass and I would watch fascinated at the effort women take to rearrange their face.

Dad, on the other side, would grumble about retrieving his rear view mirror. This would be repeated all over again as we approached Umtali.

On the return trip we would invariably stay over at the Black Mountain Inn in Cashel before taking the scenic route back to Melsetter. Eileen Botes, who owned the Inn with husband Cedric, was mums best friend.

They had met when Mum arrived into the country in 1950 with two kids and a baby and Eileen took us in.

It was quite a feat for a woman in those days to drive alone from George in the eastern Cape of South Africa to Cashel which mum did towing a trailer with all our possessions, two restless kids and a month old screaming baby strapped up in a sling swinging from inside the roof of the car.

Dad, who was a mining engineer, was in the Persian Gulf, wrapping up his Bauxite Mine that he owned on Abamusa Island.

Mum and we kids stayed at the Black Mountain Inn until Dad arrived to settle us all in our new home on the farm.

My mother, all of five feet and not to forget the half an inch, did the community thing. She taught rural women hygiene and how to make marmalade and bread in a 3 legged cauldron over a wood fire.

Her assistant and interpreter was the gross opposite. Her name was Mai Ngungunyana and she spread her cellulite over the front two seats of

Kalahari Kate, the series 1 Station Wagon Land Rover that keeled over dramatically on the passenger side. The counter balance was Mum who, despite the benefit of cushions, just managed to see through the steering wheel.

But times changed. The awakening of the Nationalist movement into an aggressive wing came to our district with the first white being murdered.

They set pine forests on fire and were caught, until they learnt the art of making time fuses comprised of matches tied to a lit cigarette and buried in grass.

The SAS were called in, driving their open Saber Land Rover's nose to tail around the Village Square and impressed the girls. They parachuted out of Dakota's in which a couple had their under slung packs entangled to each other before finally perching precariously in the heights of a gum tree on the Ashworth's farm. It was all impressive stuff for a kid.

Then our parents joined the effort. They became Police Reservists. Mum became a radio operator and Dad dressed in blue denim uniform and Second World War helmet, painted in white with Police written across the front, trained to jump out of Helicopters and man road blocks.

At school, our games changed from Cowboys and Indians to Cops and Robbers, all played out in the pine plantation above the tennis court but nobody wanted to be the robbers. Our Dads were the heroes and that's who we wanted to be.

Exeat weekends were our problem. Parents would be on call out so we would be sent to those that weren't.

I was too young to start boarding school as I would only turn 5 in November so my first year was spent with Granny Howard, a retired widow who had a house in the village.

She would pack my sandwiches and cool drink into a brown paper bag and I would walk up the hill to school every day.

At tea break I would have a collection of boarding friends wanting to share my syrup sandwiches which were a treat compared to what I eventually got as a boarder and in which it became my turn to solicit homemade sandwiches from the day scholars.

The road leading to the school followed a small gurgling stream until it found a place to form a sharp bend and head off in the opposite direction along a cutting in the embankment and up to the school.

In this valley, Eucalyptus trees grew exceedingly tall, trying to reach for the sun and in amongst them was a short cut path that crossed over the stream. It was quite eerie walking through this quiet, twilight atmosphere with only the sounds of the stream and occasional Laurie screech.

The school had no mains electricity as we know it today. Our lights came from primus spirit lamps that Sixpence, a large kitchen worker would pump the pressure up and hang them hissing away from wire hooks off the ceiling.

He would impress us with his large biceps and split his tight fitting sleeve of his white uniform as he flexed his muscle.

Ma Cloetie was the cook matron and what a lovely person she was. She was a short Afrikaans lady that her hair length came below her butt and she would Plait this into one long rope and coil it around the top of her head.

She would bake us a chocolate cake and sneak it into our dormitory for our illegal end of term midnight feast.

Her kitchen comprised a huge Aga anthracite stove with paraffin fridges and deep freezers but when the milk arrived from Gillie Bredenkamp's dairy farm near the village; it would be boiled and placed into a charcoal cooler and pick up all the flavours around, usually pickled fish and anything else revolting.

This was our tea, a tin mug of foul tasting milk that formed a skin on top. When pupils complain of their boarding school meals, trust me, believe it.

Our meals usually comprised boiled or pickled fish, boiled spinach that sometimes had the carcass of some unfortunate stink bug, boiled potatoes or mash, boiled pumpkin and for pudding, who in their right mind can enjoy tapioca, custard, bread pudding or rice pudding. I certainly didn't. What wasn't finished was stored in the charcoal cooler to further contaminate the milk.

Now a charcoal cooler is a clever contraption. It is a tall narrow cupboard that has double skin walls of bird wire. In between the bird wire, charcoal is filled from top to bottom that has water dripping through it from a drip tray placed on top of the cupboard.

Inside will be shelves to store the food and the whole thing placed outside for the breeze to blow through the moist charcoal and cooling the air. It works well and I have since made them to cool veggies when on holiday in the hot Zambezi Valley.

Liz Murray whose parents farmed on top of the hill above the Ashworth's, was another of my friends.

She and I were close in age and would play together from an early age. She was a real tom boy and the two of us together spelt trouble.

Our Kindergarten class room accommodated both KG1 and KG2 in the same room only divided by a passageway down the centre. I chose to sit with Liz at the double desk but Miss Frobisher, our teacher, could not get me to study and so split us up and put me at the front of the class under her watchful eye.

At the end of the first year, Liz moved to the KG2 section across the room and I was held back a year. This was repeated again when I was due to go into the next classroom of Std 1 and spent another year in KG 2.

By the time I entered my final year of Std 5; I had become an 'old hand' of the school and given the task of head boy of Martin House with Rosemary Atkins as head girl.

That year Martin House won the swimming gala and I had the picture of Rosemary and I holding up the cup as triumphant winners until it got burnt in the house fire years later.

That was the year I fancied myself up with brillcream in my hair in the fashion of Cliff Richards, my favorite singer.

Dad was on 'call up' and Mum had to supervise the dipping of the cattle. Dad had switched to a tractor driven spray race as being cheaper on chemicals than the conventional dip tank and consequently the tank had not been used for quite some time.

As usual, the animal health inspector would come along to inspect the cattle and on finding a few ticks, insisted that Mum put the cattle through the tank. But by this stage, the arsenical dip had oxidized and had disastrous results on the cattle.

The arsenic poisoning burnt the skin on the cattle until they became weak and died. Dad was wiped out over night and had to sell the farm to clear his debts.

There was an appalling atmosphere on the farm, rotting meat could be smelt for miles and the air was filled with circling vultures that had the feast of their lives.

It was a sad day for me when my parents picked me up from Umtali Boys High School and instead of going home, stayed at the Black Mountain Inn.

My parents were standing in for the Botes whilst they were on holiday and also looking for a job. Our beloved home in Melsetter was no more. It was sold to our neighbours who finally sold it on to the Forestry Commission.

Now, there is no evidence of any habitation, the whole farm has been planted over with pine forests.

CHAPTER TWO
UMTALI

With my years of experience at junior school, I was considered intelligent enough to progress to Umtali Boys High School and soon after, my parents left Melsetter.

They worked as relief managers for various hotels until finally getting a permanent position to run the Balmoral Hotel behind the Vaudeville Theater in Umtali, both of which were owned by Mr. Hanna.

I started high school boarding at Kopje House, which in the early days was part of the original co-ed Umtali School that encompassed the present day girl's school. It was great as I was to get my first bicycle and as a group, we would cycle to the recently constructed boy's school.

Kopje House was purely accommodation for the first year boys after which I moved into Crawford House Hostel in the main school complex. I was not there long when my parents removed me to become a day scholar living with them at the Balmoral Hotel.

The original site for Umtali was settled alongside

the banks of the Umtali River that flowed from the east escarpment and lay close to the gold mining settlement of Penalonga.

Cecil John Rhodes, the founder of Rhodesia was pushing through a railway line from the coast at Beira in Mozambique to the capital, Salisbury, situated in the middle of the country. But the engineers had great difficulty finding a route up through the escarpment that formed the border with Mozambique and have Umtali serviced by the railway.

Rhodes then compensated the settlers and asked them to re establish themselves on the southern side of the mountain range where the engineers could find an easier route for the railway line.

A wagon route was constructed over this range to reach the new site and on completion of this pass that coincided with Christmas, it became known as Christmas Pass. Thereafter, the old settlement became Old Umtali where the buildings that had been constructed were given over to the Jesuits to form a missionary station.

From the top of the Christmas Pass, one has a magnificent view of the city of Umtali spread out below in avenues of Cassia and Bohemia trees. Like Melsetter, Umtali is nestled in a basin that is open in the east and looks out over the escarpment towards the coast.

It is an important city as the gateway to the port where a large portion of the country's imports and exports are handled. With the sheltered effect of the basin, it can become quite hot in summer.

Soon after moving into Balmoral, my sister, Celia decided to go over to the United Kingdom. I was very fond of my sister to the point of possessiveness that I gave any prospective boyfriend a hard time and would rudely stare at them as they sat fidgeting in the lounge chair. No one was to take my sister away from me.

The day came that she decided to move to the United Kingdom, and I was distraught. The night she was due to catch the train to Salisbury, she had a farewell session with her friends and boyfriends and one of them decided to get me out of the way by insisting that I would enjoy a ride up Christmas Pass on the back of his Matchless 500 motorbike. It wasn't what I wanted at all at that moment and by the time I returned, Celia was safely on board the train. The decoy had worked.

I had no contact with horses other than those of Digby and Celia who had a horse each on Nyhodi and even then, was limited to Celia putting me in the saddle on her horse, Gypsy, and telling me to hold the rains whilst she prepared herself to go out on a ride. Gypsy would then put her head down to eat the lush kukuyu lawn in front of the house and I would be catapulted over her head. I didn't think this was exactly fun but I have always loved the smell of a horse.

Now at the Balmoral, I would ride on my bicycle to the Umtali Saddle Club, behind hospital hill, and chat to the horses stabled there. Denis Ford had taken notice of this and since he had become friends with my parents, persuaded them to allow me to join Bob Taylor's riding school in the Vumba Mountains, south of Umtali.

Bob Taylor was a retired Police Instructor and taught his pupils as if they were police recruits. He would collect his pupils in Umtali and we would ride in the back of his canvas canopied Commer two tonne truck up the winding Vumba road to the top and bale out feeling thoroughly car sick.

Mrs. Taylor took the beginners in a closed arena where we mounted and formed a single line, one behind the other. "Walk on" she would command and as one, the horses would obey regardless of what the rider did.

Later I progressed to Bob's class where we had the excitement of going out on a ride over the beautiful scenic views that looked over into Mozambique. But it was no different. "Trot on" he bellowed and all the horses obeyed as one and in single file. There was nothing I could do to persuade my mount to break ranks and to take our own route away from the regiment.

I was frustrated and I quit. "Told you so" said Dad "just like your brother and sister, want a horse and do nothing with it! Just a passing phase." He said with relief that he had gotten away with it.

I was back on my bicycle visiting my friends at the Saddle Club. This time, Sheila Orr suggested I contact Sheila Barry, a farmer's wife in Old Umtali that was about to start up a riding school.

Dad would not have it. "You had your chance" he said. So I brought in the big gun, Denis Ford, the one I knew who would successfully twist his arm.

Sheila Barry collected us from town, me being the only boy amongst all these gorgeous Girls High pupils. The odds looked good.

Sheila asked us how we rode. "Very well" I said. What else could I say and not lose face amongst all these girls. "Fine" she replied "take your horse over that jump."

There was nothing for it; I just had to do it. Well, the horse did, did it well, as I came bounding off in a spread eagled pile of dust. My dignity left with the horse galloping back to the stables. "Shall we start from the beginning then!" she taunted with a smile on her face.

My parents had been offered a job to run the Kariba Heights Hotel for the Rhodesia Breweries. Fred and Sheila offered to take me in and they became my new home. They had three kids, James who was a year older than me, Neil, a year younger and then Rose. Neil became my big buddy and Rose my new younger sister that I loved to bits.

Sheila was an excellent teacher and made riding so much fun. We did it all, show jumping, dressage and three phase eventing. We joined the Saddle Club and played Polocrosse, a sport I thoroughly enjoyed and played for a further forty years, playing for my country and travelling to South Africa, Australia and New Zealand.

It gave me so much that I felt duty bound to write my first book on the history of our sport in this country before any more records would get lost through the chaos of the land grab era in the 2000's.

On turning 16 I acquired my first car, a 1952 VW Beetle complete with crash gearbox and cable operated brakes that seldom synchronized the four wheels.

Coming home from School one lunch time with fellow illegal smokers, I noticed the lunch time traffic had stopped over a narrow two lane bridge but not in time to coax the car to a stop. The choice was to either rear end the last car or have a head on with the lead oncoming car.

With the right front wheel locked and screeching black rubber, I managed to squeeze a third lane and came to a standstill tightly sandwiched between the two lanes of traffic. There was no time for any of us to get rid of the cigarette evidence, besides, had we flicked them out of the window it would have entered the window of the car on our flank, they were that close.

Sadly, as it turned out, the car on our flank was my geography master Mr. Menning who could quite easily have stuck his head through my passenger window but clearly didn't want to risk asphyxiation from all the smoke that was now blending with the tyre rubber smoke. 'Pocock, what do you think you are doing' he said, as if I knew. 'See me back at school'.

Back at School I was interrogated and reprimanded but no mention was made of the smoking although he clearly knew, but nicknamed my car the 'E type VW' after the E type Jaguar sports car that was popular at the time. The name stuck.

Moving on in time, my VW was un ceremoniously removed from the road by the Vehicle Inspection Department at a road block on Christmas Pass much to the glee of Mr. Menning, but a week later was mortified when I arrived at School in my father's borrowed tank of a car, a

Jaguar Mk 7. 'Now it really is a Jag E type' he says with a heavy heart.

The Police were the bain of my life in those days, and still are. I had stopped growing sometime back and at 16 looked like a 12 year old. Only later, when I was in the army did I start growing.

They were convinced I was not mature enough or old enough to sit behind the wheel of a motor vehicle and would often hang around waiting for me to get into my car and then pounce. I would require two cushions to see through the steering wheel but a third just gave me enough elevation to give the impression of normal.

On one occasion, I was instructed by my father to go to the Bus Stop to pick up Murungupenny and Tickey and take them to the Post Office to collect money he had sent for them.

Exactly why they decided to squat on the back seat as against sit on it, I have no idea unless it was old timers respect or they just didn't know how to sit on a seat. But there it was, I'm driving up Main St with these two squatting on the seat in total amazement that the 'picinini boss' was now driving a car, when a very smart looking Cop, and they were in those days, thundered past me on his BSA 500 Motor Bike and hauled me over.

The usual rigmarole ensued but then noticed these veterans squatting on the back seat and says 'even these old buggers are ready to jump ship.'

But my VW gave me good lessons in life, one of which was mechanical as it often broke down.

After seizing the engine, I decided to upgrade to a bigger motor and a synchronized gear box that my father sourced for me off a VW Combi. The problem was the half shafts were not the same and so I had to split the gearbox to fit my old ones.

After firing up the engine for the first time I climbed into the car feeling very smug with myself and put it into 1st gear to go for a test drive. But the car shot backwards and so to in all the other forward gears. Reverse gear made it go forward and I sat there fully perplexed as to how this could happen.

Had I put the damn thing upside down! But aid came in the form of an old man with a walking stick who casually said to me. 'My boy, I made the same mistake on a Model T Ford, you have put the crown wheel the wrong way around'.

CHAPTER THREE
POLICE

As previously mentioned, Police have always been the bain of my life and nothing has changed only the efficiency and quality.

It is now Zimbabwe and we have entered a Police State. Road blocks, comprising four or five police officers position themselves in ambush positions on blind spots or intersections without warning signs and extort spot fines of usually $20 a time for anything they consider appropriate.

There is no point in arguing, it gets you nowhere and it is widely assumed that most of the money finds its way into their pockets. A very lucrative pass time.

But there is always humour where there is adversity. Driving in from Nyamandlovu to Bulawayo one late afternoon I was stopped by a Policeman who politely wanted to do a vehicle check on my 1957 series 1 Land Rover.

Everything worked accept my brake lights. On being told this I feigned ignorance and suggested he get in the car, press the brake pedal and I would go around and see for myself.

This he did and I said with a lie "my friend, they are working". "Ah" he said very surprised, "are you sure, then you may proceed".

Later, driving through Norton towards Harare the same thing occurred. This time it was my hand brake. It did work but the ratchet was worn and I had to hold the handle up whilst the policeman tried in vain to push the car.

He then noticed me holding the hand brake and said "My friend, let us pretend we are going shopping, get out of the car".

Then there was a friend, Doug Fingland who had had rather enough to drink and was still drinking his beer when he was stopped at the road block.

The Policeman said in a very knowledgeable tone, "you are not allowed to drink and drive, pull off the road and finish your beer then you may proceed."

But these were the days before the galloping inflation and they became more business related as money became scarce. Police were all over the place extorting money for phoney misdemeanours.

If in town it was a simple matter to run them as they were usually on foot with no communications or follow up procedures.

I attempted this in my Mazda Pick Up

loaded with fertilizer. I was stopped approaching a traffic light and uphill. From his body language I knew he was up to no good.

Seeing that the lights were green up ahead I decided to run it but my Mazda is not exactly quick off the mark especially with a load and the Policeman was running alongside me swearing and banging the side of my truck.

By the time I got to the lights they had turned from orange to red and I figured if I stop I was in for it, so I ducked left through the red lights and noticed in my rear view mirror that these cops had a B Car.

So going through the gears I floored it, bearing in mind that this truck has no Speedo but a calendar, and ducked into the avenues.

Of course they will not follow me, why have the hassle and lose out on potential revenue still to come.

I was hired by my neighbour John Naested to collect his Stamp Mill in my lorry from Kwe Kwe. It was approaching Christmas and the police were out in force to collect their dues.

Stopped at a road block at Turn Pike Service Station, before Norton, I was told to pull over and join the huge number of vehicles waiting to be fleeced. I behaved and waited but soon got impatient and left.

Approaching Kadoma, two towns away, I noticed a very overloaded and clapped out car struggling to overtake me so I politely tapped off to let him pass.

As he did so, and in synchronized motion, two yellow armlets appeared from either side back windows and waved as any graceful swan could do and gave the impression the car was trying to fly.

The police had found some initiative and jumped the next car at the road block. He tells me he is taking me back to Norton and locking me up for running a road block.

I say, "Come on now, we all know the game, how much?"

"Ah", he says, "are you bribing a police officer!"

"Yes" I replied, "that is the system."

"So how much" he grumbles.

"Five hundred million" I think I said, remember it is inflation.

Horrified, he rejects this and so we negotiate a mutual figure. I proceed while they hitch hike back to their road block.

CHAPTER FOUR
UDI AND NATIONAL SERVICE

In 1965 Ian Smith, the Prime Minister of Rhodesia declared unilateral independence [U.D.I] from Great Britain. Sanctions were imposed and Harold Wilson figured it would take a short time to bring Rhodesia to its knees.

But sanctions proved to be the catalyst that brought all white Rhodesians, even those that did not support U.D.I, together.

As a country, we were reliant on imports from the UK but sanctions changed all that. Companies started up and made replacement items, albeit rough and ready to begin with, but soon the quality would emerge.

Unwittingly, Harold Wilson, the UK Prime Minister, galvanized the country behind Ian Smith.

Fuel was to be our problem. The British Royal Navy set up a blockade around Beira to prevent tankers off loading fuel destined for Rhodesia. But South Africa came to our aid and so did the Portuguese in Mozambique.

Fuel rationing was introduced and whilst the allocation was tight, it was an orderly system resulting in no queues at the service stations.

Coupons, crudely printed on news print would be issued and it says a lot for the unity of purpose in everyone that forgery, so easily done, was not an issue.

We in Umtali were fortunate being on the border of Mozambique. The Portuguese set up a fuel station at the border for the benefit of Rhodesians and with the duty removed, made the fuel price cheap.

Over weekends or holidays I would fill up both tanks on the Jag and with a bunch of school friends, head on to Manica town to their Olympic size swimming pool and ate prawns and Portuguese bread and smoked honey flavoured cheroots.

Of course a visit to the wine merchant in town was a must to try out all their free samples.

Zapu, the African Nationalist movement that had started in the 50's under Joshua Nkomo initially and then joined by Zanu under Ndabaningi Sithole, started to intensify the guerrilla bush war with backing and training from countries such as Russia and China. Independent Zambia and Botswana were to be used as spring boards to infiltrate Rhodesia.

The war had increased to the point where it was no longer a civil police issue alone but took on more of a military role. The government introduced national conscription and increased its regular army.

The police hybridized into a Para military role with the formation of anti tracking reserve unit as well as the support unit amongst others.

With the increase of military activity, national service increased from four and a half months to nine months. The extra time after basic training was to be spent on border patrols along the Zambezi River that divides Zambia from Rhodesia.

I was 20 when I finally went to do my national service. Mostly it was straight from school unless you had an exemption to attend university or college.

I had hoped to go to Gwebi Agricultural College but as I had failed my English exam meant rewriting it in Salisbury. Instead I took on a Job with the Sugar Refineries.

Arriving at Heany Junction by steam train, we were hustled into Lorries bound for Llewellyn Barracks where our civilian independent personalities were transformed over night into one unified amoeba. We were paraded, not knowing each other, outside the tin barrack rooms where our first roll call took place.

Each surname was called out in alphabetical order and I waited nervously for my turn when the

P's came around. 'Fuckpig' the staff sergeant bellowed out. No one answered and I thought, who on earth would have a name like that. 'Pocock', he bellowed finally. And there it was, I was now fuckpig for the rest of my training.

I had a huge drawback. Despite being older than most of the recruits, I still looked under age. I would require an ID if I wanted a beer from a pub on our infrequent weekend passes and here I was 20years old.

Cross country runs were designed to single out those who fell by the wayside and they would be transferred to HQ positions. I could ill afford this; my character would never recover from this and would be driven into insignificance. Despite raw blistered feet I was determined to hang in there.

But my late development in life was about to turn around for the better. Shortly I would be able to shave real hair instead of going through the motions in amongst the row of grizzly recruits in the wash room.

Barrack room inspections were nightmares. Being exhausted from the day before, we had to rise at an ungodly hour to prepare the barrack room.

Floors had to be polished and shining, stick boots spooned and glistening and our bed clothing had to be folded in perfect squares that were in rank with everyone else's.

It didn't take long to short circuit the system and sleep in a sleeping bag next to the bed and on the floor.

We were all required to have our 3 in 1 jabs known as TAB. A women nurse was training nervous young national service medics to administer the jabs. As usual we formed up in alphabetical order and instead of joining the F's I preferred to keep to my slot of Fuckpig with a P. By the time I got there the nurse was in a state of frustration.

She yelled at the learner medic as he thrust the needle into my arm "this is a skinny bugger so don't push the needle right through him" where upon he quickly removed it half way through the dose and went for a second attempt. I wobbled out of the clinic and promptly passed out.

Finally the training came to an end and we were now fighting machines ready to be deployed to the border. A passing out parade party was held consisting of a braai and beers.

A couple of warm beers, I like them warm, got me pretty well oiled and presented the right opportunity for my staff sergeant to present me one that was slightly warmer.

After a healthy slug I discovered that this wasn't beer but freshly bottled pee.... but more importantly, he now renamed me Pocock and

Fuckpig became a thing of the past. I had made it and now my Staff Sergeant was a friend instead of the dreaded enemy I had wished to shoot in the back, as I doubled alone around the parade square with rifle above my head.

Morally, employers were required to pay their employees whilst they were on military call up. I had heard through the grape vine that my employer, the sugar refineries, had fired all their young white staff and replaced them with black staff. Blacks were not subject to call up.

Having completed my nine months of military call up I reported for work in Salisbury to see what my fate was. It was true, they had fired my work mates but surprisingly I had been promoted to the new position of Assistant Factory Manager to control four pack supervisors against the two that we had.

My bank account had nine months worth of salaries and now I had received an increase with my promotion. Not a bad situation to have.

Chris Pocock

CHAPTER FIVE
SALISBURY

I had left Sugar Refineries and done a short stint as a farm assistant in Norton. The promised bonus had not materialized and disgruntled I left to work for Lyons Brooke Bond as a leaner factory manager in the Ice Cream department.

Six months later I was promoted to factory manager to start up the new section of Squash factory producing drink concentrates and the Farm House range of chutneys and sauces.

My boss, Mr. Rose the managing director, was the old school upper class gentleman that rode to work in the back seat of his white Cadillac chauffeur driven car.

He called me into his office one day and asked me to produce a new line of Melba sauces to compliment the Lyons range of ice creams. One was to be chocolate and the other strawberry. Always willing to please I ran off to produce the samples for his professional opinion.

Once approved I started production and the new products were filled into white plastic bottles and distributed around a selected market.

It wasn't long before the phones started

ringing with disgruntled merchants complaining that the chocolate bottles were exploding and leaving a sticky mess over their shelves.

All were returned and I was summoned to the big boss for a reprimand. "It's your hygiene" he bellowed, "Sort it out!"

And so I did. The factory was cleared and scrubbed from wall to wall; finger nails inspected and face masks worn. The place smelt and looked like a hospital.

Out came the next batch and left in the warehouse for a while to see what would happen. Nothing, so off to market it went. But it wasn't long before the dreaded phone calls started again. Chocolate smeared distributors were not happy.

I could not believe this was happening but with the strawberry being ok I started to figure the odd one out was the acid to react with the preservative.

Strawberry had citric acid but the chocolate had none. I wanted to put a small amount in the chocolate but my boss would not go along with my thinking and refused. So I made up two unmarked bottles, one with and one without and took it up to his office to see if he could identify which was the illegal one. He couldn't and I got the go ahead.

The next batch stood the test of time and the launch went ahead with a nervous strawberry strapped to the chocolate around the middle with a sticker proclaiming, '2 for the price of 1'.

Nothing happened and I was back in the Boss's good books until one Monday morning he arrived to work in a filthy mood and I was summoned to his office.

He loved to hold pompous dinner parties and the products of his company were proudly used. Ice Cream was a given but nobody noticed the chocolate melba bottle swollen like a rugby ball until some dear lady shook it before pouring the contents on to her ice cream.

With the shake, it raised enough energy to explode and spray everyone with sour tasting chocolate.

The evidence was thrust before me, a fragmented sticky piece of plastic that fortunately the code bar was still readable. It proved to be an old batch and my job was saved.

At this time, I was renting a small cottage in Arcturus on Pete Clark's farm, a farming community fifty kilometers east of Salisbury. I could not live in town and had to have my medicinal country scenery.

I would commute to work on an old BSA Bantam motor bike until I got fed up with riding for hours in the rain and cold.

I splashed out and bought a second hand Borguard motor car that only its mother and I could love for it was a collection of nuts and bolts and disarranged panels.

My maiden voyage home, I pulled into the shopping centre and filled the tank with petrol and did my bachelor grocery shopping of beers, cigarettes, tinned Vienna's and grapefruit, then proceeded home.

Driving along the narrow tar road down a slope, flames suddenly erupted from under the bonnet and by the time the brakes decided to work and bring the car to a halt, the whole damn thing was ablaze.

I escaped without my groceries and remembering that the tank was full, I sprinted up the road before it exploded.

I sat in the middle of the road and watched my investment melt before my eyes, waiting for the holly wood style explosion but it didn't happen. Instead, a full tank of petrol simply fed the fire until the car was hardly recognizable.

A man in a VW Beetle rushed off to the nearby cement factory and gathered fire extinguishers and in his dubious wisdom called the fire brigade. The fire extinguishers had no effect.

Shortly the sound of two sirens as a Land Rover and fire truck from the Salisbury Fire Department pulled up in a professional manner.

Two men grabbed the canvas hose and charged towards their molten pray, signaling as they went to fire up the pump.

But the pump refused to fire. A tickle here and a tickle there and with a pull on the rope it grudgingly sprang to life.

The two on the other end braced themselves for the rush of water and opened the tap. But it only dribbled out. Engine cut, pump primed and away they went dousing the remaining flames to reveal a steaming blob of molten metal.

The sound of another siren signaled a police B car speeding towards us. The white patrol officer wanted details. Was the car licensed and insured he demanded, to which I untruthfully confirmed.

He then scratched around the car with a stick to see if he could find the license disc, but that wasn't there in the first place and he was not going to know that.

Finally, a third flashing light brought the arrival of a Thames Trader wrecker with 'Arians Truck Breakers' printed on the side. He had come to collect the carcass and take it, with me, to my cottage on the farm.

Bills arrived in the post; I had to pay the Salisbury Municipality for the efficient fire engines and Arians for providing the hearse.

CHAPTER SIX
QUE QUE

I went back farming as I had had enough of working in a big city. I worked for Jeremy and Sonia Fisher below Christian Bank north of Salisbury on St Gerera Farm and loved the work and lifelong friendship that came from it.

The Fishers moved to South Africa and I was to start a new job with Mike McGrath in Horseshoe but my old boss Mr. Rose from Lyons made me an offer I could not refuse and that was to build and then run a tomato paste factory on a farm outside Que Que.

Que Que is just short of half way and 200 km south west of Salisbury on the main road to Bulawayo, the second Capital City to Salisbury. It is a town that supplies the big mines in the area as well as the surrounding cattle ranches.

Lyons Brooke Bond had joined a farming syndicate that had a large irrigation farm on the border of Jombe Communal Lands some 40km north west of Que Que on the Gokwe dirt road. It had an earth dam that could irrigate 400 acres of land and I was to build my factory close to it.

The idea was that I would recruit out growers from around the district with the syndicate farm being one under their farm manager.

The factory went up fairly quickly and the processing plant installed. We would take the short bushy variety of tomato that was fleshy and ideal to concentrate into paste and puree and pack it into 5kg cans for the export catering market.

My problem was getting growers to produce tomatoes for me as there was a lucrative market in table tomatoes that commanded a higher price. Vendors would arrive from Salisbury and Bulawayo and purchase these by the lorry load.

The crop grown on the farm failed and I was dependant on Mr. Bull who was a consistent producer from the opposite side of Que Que in the Rhodesdale Block.

I spoke to Mr. Rose on his visit and suggested he negotiate a section of the irrigation and allow me to grow tomatoes for the factory.

He then gave me a budget to purchase a tractor and equipment and we started growing for ourselves. This gave us sufficient tomatoes to run a double shift and cans of tomato paste were heading across the border to South Africa.

I had no house at the factory, that, I would build later, but in the mean time I rented a house on Basil Scheeper's farm next door.

Dad had died in December, 1974, the previous year whilst I was in the army and Celia looked after Mum. She had broken her leg and Celia, being a nurse, took good care of her. Now Celia felt it was my turn to shoulder my responsibilities so Mum moved in with me.

I was a bachelor and lived like one. I had my bed, stove and fridge as essentials but the rest was arbitory chairs and Lyon's empty tea chests as tables. Mum was shocked, came to town with me and kitted out the house with new furniture.

One day she hobbled down the passageway on her crutches, opened the door that lead into the kitchen and walked straight into the back end of my horse. "What on earth is this horse doing in the kitchen!" she said after recovering her composure. "It's raining Mum and I have no stables and I am not shoeing her in the rain."

It was a huge strain having Mum live with me who in her bossy way, tried to change my life style.

My girlfriend at the time, Barbara, was similar in size and temperament and the two did not hit it off. They fought like cat and dog until I couldn't take it anymore and my only choice was to break up with Barbara. Squeaky tits was my mother's endearing name for her.

I made friends with Basil Scheepers who had taken on the job as mine manager down the road.

I was in town buying building material and phoned Basil to come over to dinner. When I got back, I received a call from a rancher closer to Que Que that my two dogs were hunting on his property.

One was a recently acquired dog and I discovered he was a habitual hunter and took my dog along with him. I was annoyed as it meant driving all the way back to near Que Que before taking the branch road of nearly the same distance.

By the time I arrived back, Basil was waiting for me and I told him the story "Why don't you shoot the damn dog for me?" I stormed as I disappeared into the house.

No sooner had I said it than I heard a gunshot. "What are you doing?" I said in amazement. "You said shoot it!" he replied. "I didn't mean it and besides, you have shot the wrong dog!" Dinner was very quiet that night.

Alan and Eleanor Lowe ranched on my side of Que Que on Sessombi Ranch on the banks of the Sebakwe River. They were good to me and made me welcome in their home. Alan was a very popular man in the district, had a lovely happy disposition and was a national legend in Polocrosse. To me he was a mentor.

Sitting on the veranda overlooking the Sebakwe River, beer in hand, he told me about his Arab Stallion that he had bought some nine years before.

He ran this stallion on the ranch to improve the blood lines of his mares that he was breeding from. He told me that this horse was highly schooled and knew a few circus tricks but that he hadn't backed it since he bought it many years ago. I suggested we go and try.

Alan had him in a halter and tried to remember how to get him to do these tricks. It had been some years since he was shown.

The stallion was clearly trying to understand these confused signals, curtsying down on one front leg, then stand up on his hind legs. Eventually he became annoyed and flew at Alan, biting a nasty hole in his chest.

I got on his back and through just leg aids had him responding to all the aids. I could not believe how intelligent this animal was and the fact that he remembered so clearly all these aids after all those years running free on the ranch.

Rhodesdale, on the other side of Que Que was made up of cattle ranchers with some doing cropping. They had a small club and I played Polocrosse there.

The distance one way was about 80km for me so I would load my horses in my Isuzu truck on a Saturday morning, play Polocrosse in the afternoon and sleep the horses there overnight to play again the next morning.

We would have a good social in the pub that night and when everyone left to go home, we from the other side, would be given the keys, told to write down the drinks we had, then throw sleeping bags down on the floor and spend the night in the pub.

It was a great community. Ken and Sandy King ranched just down the road from the club and Ken, a great character that is always full of pranks is probably the only guy I know that when dressed up as a women looks quite stunning with his blue eyes.

At a Polocrosse dance he had one guy all amorous as he seduced him dancing around the floor. For us in the know it was hilarious and when this poor guy realized he was being watched, suddenly pushed Ken away saying "Someone, get this crazy woman off me."

Now in the 70's, there were no dating agencies or adverts for partners in the personal columns. It just wasn't considered right to do such a thing but the South African Farmers Weekly ran a regular Hitching Post column that we Rhodesians were bemused by.

I decided to put an advert in the Que Que
Times to see what reaction I got, it went like this.
YOUNG VIRILE FARMER SEEKS WIFE.
Candidates must qualify in the following.
A good ability to weather forecast
Good in labour control
Knowledge in animal husbandry
Sound mechanical aptitude
Good knowledge in electrics
Applicants should apply, with photograph [of
tractor]
To
B.A. Failed
P.O. Box ….
Que Que.

The replies I got were stimulating. One had
given birth to twelve children and felt amply
qualified at labour control.

Another had had four husbands and had
recognized the animal in each of them.

One signed V.D. Passed.

But quite a number had applied for a
genuine relationship and sent pictures of
themselves, a few of which were a close
resemblance to a tractor.

Not doing your national service was social suicide at

that time. Draft dodgers and conscientious objectors were not tolerated and generally would have to leave the country.

My friend Simon Rick was genuinely nervous of doing his call up and largely because his very protective mother would not have her son 'die for the cause'. I tried to persuade him to either join the Police or the Internal Affairs Department and get an office job.

He was not convinced and he suffered appalling humiliation and abuse from the Que Que community.

We went to a dance at the Que Que hotel. I had a date and with Simon and another friend, Paul Savory, we had a pleasant time.

Eventually we relaxed in the lounge and I took the opportunity to go for a pee. Paul came running in to the toilet to tell me that Simon was being beaten up, 'come quick' he said.

I came out to find half a dozen men chasing around the lounge with Simon ducking around furniture to avoid the mob, just as in a pub fight in a western movie. I stepped in, the knight to the rescue, and got planted by a short stocky guy.

Simon gallantly rescued my date and locked themselves in the car.

The mob is out to teach me a lesson and I focus on the short stocky guy so that I wouldn't be lonely in hospital.

Paul, not physically able to contribute much, climbed in for all his worth and the fighting eventually stopped.

The Manager and bouncer come along and told me to stop the fighting or they would call the Police. "If you want to stop the fight" I said, "you had better do so."

The minute they left, the mob grabbed Paul and shoved him into the corner of the fireplace and started beating him. Again, the knight to the rescue.

This time the girlfriends joined in and I took severe punishment from handbags, hair pulling and clothes torn whilst the men continued beating me.

Pinned to the floor they proceeded to kick me until a brave man in civilian clothes ran in shouting, 'stop the fight, I am police'. The mob then dropped me and chased after him.

One of the mob was rolling on the floor clutching his leg that he had broken, I presume from kicking me, but the girlfriends blamed it on me and proceeded to give me another bashing with their handbags.

Some years later, at a Polocrosse tournament at the Rhodesdale club, Paul called me from the bar and reminded me of this incident.

The mob was in the Marquee and wanted to meet me, broken leg guy included. We recounted the incident and laughed and had a great party in memory of it all.

Simon skipped the country after that but quite some time later he returned to the border and handed himself over.

He opted to do the safer thing and joined Internal Affairs hoping for that office job. With the war escalating it was not to be and Simon found himself in the heat of things and survived being blown up in a land mine, drove through an ambush and defended serious attacks on the protected village he was administering.

It was a huge personality transformation for him and he came back to Que Que a hero.

At about this time I was looking to buy a new horse and had answered an advert for one that I think belonged to a show jumper or dressage rider.

Either way I didn't know this person but turned up in Borrowdale to try it out. I was scrutinized and grilled if I was a suitable person to be the custodian of her horse.

Finally she wanted to know how well I rode before she allowed me to mount. By now the devil had gotten into me and I convinced her of my excellence as a horseman and was allowed to mount.

Having secured my stirrups I put the horse straight into a cantor, grabbed the reigns in my left fist that I held high, and the right anywhere I thought I needed balance and bounced about in the saddle like a novice that little of me was making contact.

To add insult to injury, I twisted around in the saddle insecurely and told her that her horse was not good enough.

As you can imagine, I did not get to buy the horse and today wonder if, whoever she is, will ever get to read this book.

Yet another horse story around this time was when I sold a horse to a friend, Eric Phillips who farmed in Glendale.

To get the horse there he borrowed my car and horse box and in return lent me his Sunbeam sports car that had quick release spoked wheels.

I rather fancied driving around town in this open top sports car and approaching the Avondale traffic lights I changed down through the gears in a noisy 'look at me' fashion…… And my back wheels fell off with the car landing on the tar in an embarrassing screech.

Eric had omitted to warn me not to use the gears to slow down as it required the acceleration to tighten the faulty hubs.

CHAPTER SEVEN
GREY SCOUTS

Harold Wilson had failed to bring Ian Smith to his knees as he had predicted. Instead Rhodesia was flourishing.

All Industry had taken up the challenge and teams of selected 'sanctions busters' were deployed to open up discreet markets around the world.

Talks would follow talks but the deadlock would not release. Wilson wanted black majority rule but Smith was adamant that the British Government had reneged on its promise of independence based on the 1962 constitution of a qualified franchise for the vote.

The Nationalist movements based in Zambia were putting on the political pressure and the war was escalating.

Territorial troops were no longer kept from the front line and casualties were mounting. New units sprung up, mounted infantry, motorbike unit and Selous Scouts amongst others.

The Selous Scouts started off as a valuable intelligence gathering unit working behind the lines as pseudo guerillas'.

I left 1st Battalion Rhodesia Regiment to join the experimental horse mounted unit. We were given a piece of vacant land at Inkomo Barracks and the horses supplied to us came from South Africa through the friends of Rhodesia foundation.

These animals had not been saddle broken and were quite unused to handling. Some of the guys brought their own horses but for the rest of us, it was a mad scramble to select the horse of our choice. Squadron Sergeant Major Ken Till had other ideas and would have none of it and allocated the horses himself.

Being typical army, the first chore was to spit and polish these woolen monsters into something like shine.

Tethered to anchor posts by a double thick bull halter with two ropes these animals could do the most amazing contortions to get even with their handler.

I watched a young Irish lad contain his quick temper, ducking the kicks whilst trying to remove the heavy growth of winter coat. We waited and watched as it was only a matter of time before his temper snapped.

Eventually the horse managed a nip on his

butt and this was the moment of truth.

The guy walked away about twenty paces from the horse lines in exasperation, rubbing his butt as he went. Stopped and reflected for a moment, then fully flushed, turned around and sprinted towards the back end of the horse and gave it a mighty kick up the butt.

In one motion, the surprised animal leapt over the cross bar in front ending up with his head pulled down to his knees by the bull halter.

Our friend took advantage of this trapped position to complete the grooming in that manner that defies belief that anything had happened.

I had not been so lucky in the horse allocation. I had been given Oakley, a sophisticated name for an animal that looked like a mule and 'mules became his nickname.

He was stubborn and arrogant as a mule and only grudgingly did he condescend to do anything, like going forward. With a bit of persuasion from a stirrup leather he would run backward and position himself under a pole or branch and only then did he buck.

My mates on the other hand had all the fun, hanging onto their steeds as they bucked and cavorted around with some landing up in hospital. Mules was quite happy to be an arm chair and watch the entertainment.

We were never designed to be a Cavalry unit but rather ground troops that used the mobility of the horse to cover ground quickly and engage the enemy. At this point the horse would be released and standard engagement tactics would apply.

Since the horse would leave the scene of action it was important to have all that you need strapped to your body and less essentials would go into the saddle bags.

Together with rifle, radio and ammunition made for a heavy and awkward load to have to dismount from your horse at the gallop and this aspect required training to get it right.

The reader's mind will boggle at the sight of a line of troops galloping onto target and with the enemy opening up with blank cartridges and witnessing pregnant troops dismount in all manner of distorted positions, some of which about faced at the sound of gun fire before the trooper could extract himself.

Some of course took the short route and flew over the horse's head as it applied hurried brakes. But all of this could result in a section leader facing the enemy alone as his troop had scattered in disarray all over the country side. Not a happy situation and required a lot of rehearsal and injuries to get it right and effective.

At the end of our training period we were required to put on a display of a mock battle to show off our tactics to all the Army's Generals.

The world's press was invited to witness the birth of Rhodesia's new fighting unit and at the end, a very brave BBC cameraman asked if he could have an action shot of riders peeling either side of him with FN rifles aimed at him.

This was organized on the very dusty piece of ground that was used as our Polocrosse field. Half a dozen riders lined up and immediately a tote sprung up to see who had the fastest horse.

With the cameraman positioned in centre field, starting orders commenced and the line of riders took off at the gallop.

From my position at the rear and under a tree, I lost visual of the riders as they disappeared in a cloud of dust, but shortly I see a rider somersault above the dust cloud only to disappear again.

He had been bucked off and landed right in front of the camera. This was a chap from Featherston, I think, who wore glasses and these glasses had dislodged from his head.

Being now quite blind, he was oblivious to the camera that was still rolling and sitting in the talcum powder dust he proceeded to look for his glasses by brail, reaching out into the dust until he found them.

Having done this he methodically cleaned them huffing onto the lenses as he did, then satisfied, he put them on, looked up and saw the camera still rolling on him for the world to see. Embarrassed, he leapt up and sprinted into hiding.

Men are generally gregarious creatures by nature and in the army, you see it more. Our toilet in those early days at Inkomo was a long drop trench with a dozen or so wooden box seats covering the trench. Around this was a hastily strung up piece of hessian that reached shoulder height when sitting on a box.

This was a useful indicator if anyone was on the throne and everyone would wait until he came out before going yourself. It therefore made no sense having all these boxes.

But by the end of the camp, inhibitions had gone to the wind and one could see a row of heads occupying all the seats, engaged in conversation and passing around the Scope magazine.

Study men at the urinal and you will see the nature of the beast. His personality is often connected to his penis and you find the insecure chap will bury himself in the corner and hold it with two hands thereby leaving it all to speculation.

The show off will select centre stage, flop it out and spray everyone's shoes as he leans on the wall with his hands and humming a tune as he sways gently on his legs.

Then after a hip shake, do up the zip rocking on his toes as he does, then a final fart to complete the exercise. He will be the one to depart with "Cheers boys" as the custodian of grandeur.

But the scary guy is the one who grunts as he undoes not only the zip but his belt as well, as he splays his legs. One has visions of this enormous thing about to fall out and into the very trough itself and suck it dry, then spray everywhere as any respectable elephant would do.

At the end of our training, the next exercise was to test the endurance of the horse so we loaded all our kit and horses onto the train and headed for Umtali.

On arrival the next morning we were told to mount up and look smart. We were to parade down Main Street where the Mayor was to give us the freedom of the city.

After basing up for the night at the show grounds we started our ride to Chipinga some 120 miles away the next morning.

Spending constant time with ones horse is a sure way to bond and Mules and I certainly did that and became firm friends with the past put firmly behind us.

The tedium of the long ride gave me the opportunity to teach him to 'rock and roll' when a friend, Graeme Crook, and I sang Elvis Presley's song 'Blue suade shoes'.

Being a narrow girthed horse I was able to hook my feet under his upper arm front legs and alternate each leg by lifting them with my feet that he pranced as good as any circus horse. Eventually he connected the song to the dance.

By the time we arrived at the Umvumvumvu river bridge where we set up overnight camp, 'Mules' was so attached to me he was like a dog and followed me everywhere.

Here was my chance to show off. I decided not to tie him up on the picket line but to let him sleep next to my sleeping bag, un tethered, bragging that he would never leave my side.

Well, he didn't. Instead he decided to join me and I woke fully trapped inside my sleeping bag with him, quite comfortably snuggled up to me.

The problem was I couldn't shift him, my arms and legs were trapped and he wasn't going to listen to my chastising. Eventually I had to call the guard to chase him off.

We were told the Chipinga town folk had organized a reception for us so from our scraggily mob, we had to form up and once again look smart for our entrance.

One of our members was a jockey turned auctioneer by the name of Peter Lovemore. During the ride he complained bitterly that his backside was sore and went on about it ad nauseam like the auctioneer that he was.

Coming into town we see a transformed Peter Lovemore, riding the front of the column, with a happy smile and acknowledging the crowds with a regal wave as though the whole exercise had been but a simple hack.

Mules had very weak and small hindquarters that proved a problem every time we climbed a hill. Everything wanted to slide off his back and so I had to rig up a breast plate to stop this happening.

He also refused to jump anything preferring to step over no matter how big the obstacle.

On patrol one day, we came across a gully that was not particularly wide but was very deep and bottomed out in a sharp 'vee'.

Everyone jumped their horses over but I knew Mules would not jump. So taking him up to the edge for him to see the danger in it, we had a long discussion as to what I expected of him.

Then taking him back a fair distance I galloped him at it with the theory that if he decided not to jump, the momentum would carry us over.

As he got to the point of take off and he

was about to jump, he changed his mind and decided to stretch.

He crashed into the embankment on the other side and the two of us, in our separate ways, headed for the bottom of the gulley, he wedging himself in the vee upside down.

It took most of the day to right him, and then walk him a long distance down the gulley for him to climb out.

In time, the unit proved itself in contact and the army moved in bulldozers and builders and built us a respectable head quarters at Inkomo Barracks. We also changed our name to Grey Scouts.

The Grey's were very successful in their roll during the war but after our initial Commanding Officer was replaced by an American who claimed 'experience in seven wars', recruiting was carried out without due selection and the unit dropped seriously in quality albeit in quantity.

He was fired and replaced with a disciplinarian that was the CO of the School of Infantry. He removed half the unit on paper and the other half were recalled for reselection and basic training.

So back to digging trenches, cross country runs and diving into an iced swimming pool that turned your balls inside out as soon as you hit the water.

We had a guy, John Davidson, a big bloke and a character that always managed to get his toes trodden on by a horse and thus confined to camp.

This time, unbelievably, he seduced this CO to allow him to erect a canteen tent that was well stocked with booze and have social evenings. No one else could achieve that nor have the guts to try.

On one occasion a pantomime was done of 'Who killed Cock Robin', but in the pigeon language that was the common communicator between the African and the European known as chilapalapa.

'Cocky Robin' would be soberly hung from a stick that was carried on the shoulders of two pall bearers.

In full military funereal spirit, everyone was dressed in number one's, squad brought to attention and presented arms before the procession slow marched into the church [canteen] were the service of who killed Cocky Robin would commence.

It was hilarious but the solemnity of the occasion was attempted to be adhered to.

But before the ceremony could commence, a cocky robin was required so Bruno Rabie was tasked to shoot a dove.

Whilst stalking one side of the tree he was not aware of the CO, who happened to be a bird lover, was on the other side studying the very same dove with binoculars. To the C.O's sudden shock, the bird fell off its perch and hit the ground at his feet, slain by a pellet gun.

Talking of doves, I tell this story that I am probably ashamed of. We were based at Manama Mission in the south west of the country. I had done extra time so did not go back with my troop but had to wait for the resupply truck.

The last days I could not go out on patrol but stayed back in base and became thoroughly bored to tears.

I had noticed that hundreds of doves would congregate where the horse cubes had been spilt so I came up with the idea of attaching a thunder flash to the end of a full role of cortex that I painstakingly knotted at short intervals. Each knot is explosive.

This length of cortex I wrapped around in a spiral with the thunder flash in the eye to a diameter of about three meters. To the end of the cortex I attached a detonator with the flex only just reaching my hiding place behind a hedge and the whole killing ground was camouflaged with sand and horse cubes.

As I lay patiently, hundreds of doves arrived over the area to settle down to gorge themselves.

There was an almighty blast that surprised me by its velocity as I touched the wires to the battery. Flying horse cubes shattered windows and a cloud of dust mushroomed over the whole place.

No one had been aware of my dirty deed and every one in camp sprinted to action stations.

Owen Fitzroy, our OC at that time was working peacefully in his ops tent before it nearly blew away.

Fortunately, he was too shocked to consider court martial and I was let off lightly with a reprimand but secretly, I think he was quite pleased at the instantaneous reaction of his troop to man stations.

I was convinced I had killed several hundred doves, but there was nothing there except three stark naked doves on the periphery that stood in shock with not a feather of clothing on.

I guess the blast had thrown them into the air, as, for the rest of the day there were doves flying around minus tail feathers crashing into trees as they negotiated to land in branches.

One chap tried the telephone line, grabbed tight and spun in circles around the wire.

They were all glad to see the back of me including the doves.

CHAPTER EIGHT
HORSESHOE

I left Que Que to finally join Mike McGrath in his farming operation in the Horseshoe Block.

I had the ambition of owning my own farm and the Agricultural Finance Corporation would not assist me without tobacco experience. Mike was an excellent and successful tobacco farmer and Charolais cattle breeder having bought his farm at the age of nineteen.

There is a fault line that starts on the edge of the escarpment in the north of the country and runs south all the way through Zimbabwe and through South Africa.

It is a range of mountains known as the Great Dyke and generally devoid of trees but is pock marked along its length with chrome mines that it is rich in.

Where it breaks away from the escarpment in the north, it turns in a near circle forming the shape of a horseshoe before heading south and within that circle is the Horseshoe farming block, hence the name.

Predominately sand veldt, it has ideal soils and altitude for the production of flue cured Virginia Tobacco.

With this location being close to Zambia, it was affected by the war from the beginning as guerillas would enter the country through the Zambezi Valley and target farming communities along the top of the escarpment.

Farmers were then required to join the Police Anti Tracking Unit [PATU] to help protect their own areas and Mike would provide his privately owned Cessna airplane for air support.

The cottage that I lived in was a lovely thatched bachelor bed sit with a small out house as a kitchen and the Horse Shoe loop road came past it with the barns, workshop and cattle handling facilities on the other side.

Part of my job was to shoot a cow once a month for rations to the workers but on this particular occasion Mike was going to shoot it.

Unfortunately for Mike, the local PATU stick on patrol came along the road and stopped the truck to watch the do being done and with the usual teasing banter.

Mike knew he could not afford to make a mistake and hope to live it down, so on his haunches he took careful aim and successfully dropped the cow in one shot.

The onlookers applauded and Mike was smug…. until the herd boy ran up and said, "You have shot the wrong cow, it was supposed to be that one!" As you see, he still hasn't lived that down.

I arrived with my two tonne Isuzu horse truck that I ferried my horses around in but it was not a user friendly vehicle to have.

Objecting to start on the battery I would have to park it on a slope for a run start and then it would obligingly fart a cloud of black smoke and kick into action.

Loaded, it tended to boil easily and I have been known to replace the head gasket on the side of the road on route to somewhere.

As bachelors, my friend Alex Anderson and I decided we needed to have girls out for weekend parties.

My bachelor pad was the answer so we would erect a tarpaulin to the front of the cottage, throw some hay bales around for seats and we had a dance hall.

The problem was to find girls to complete the event.

We rigged my truck up with a canvas canopy over the horse frame and with hay bales for seats and a cooler box of drinks we would head into town, some 150km away, and round up volunteers from the Nurses and Teachers college.

In they would pile and after a helpful push to start the truck we would return home to much joviality.

The sight that appeared out of the back of that truck was a sight to behold. They were black from head to toe with only the whites of their eyes and teeth gleaming through a faceless body.

Into the shower for a scrub down and they were as good as new and with all the local bachelors, the party would begin.

Of course we couldn't do this too often so Alex and I would go in for a night on the town.

On this particular occasion we went in his car and partied to the early hours of the morning.

The war was on and nobody travelled on the roads at night for fear of ambush, but we figured no self respecting 'gook' as we called them, would wait up in the early hours of the morning for a chance customer.

Approaching the grid that left the Commercial farming area and entering the communal area, Alex said "Watch out for cattle on the road, I don't want to ding my car".

I was fiddling with the tape deck to put on another song when I looked up and saw this big black trek ox square in front of us.

It was too late; I watched as this beast slid up the bonnet, its big horns about to pierce the windscreen on my side but then get tossed onto the road as Alex jammed on the brakes.

The ox staggered off into the bush and I was convinced it had broken a leg.

Alex is fussing over the bent front end of his car and I decided to follow the ox and put it out of its misery with my service 9 mm pistol that we all carried.

It was deep into the bush before I managed to get the final shot in and came back to the car feeling I had done the Samaritan thing.

The next morning an old man came to the farm to ask why I had shot the animal. "It had a broken leg" I said. "No", he replied, "there was nothing wrong with it". I had to compensate him.

Polocrosse was a prominent sport in our district and played at the Horseshoe Country Club, which Mike, as a dab hand in design and building, constructed with a Spanish theme. There were three fields and Horseshoe would hold the annual Easter Polocrosse tournament.

Polocrosse is a derivative of Polo that goes back some 2000 years and which evolved through twelve variations of the sport.

Polo is recognized as a hard ball being hit down the field by a mallet but in its fifth variation, around the Byzantine period, they tried using a soft ball that was picked up and thrown using a loose strung racket.

This variation then spread across Asia to Japan and up into Russia and the Ukraine in its various interpretations of play.

In 1869 it arrived in the United Kingdom with the 10th Hussars who used it in India as a military riding exercise, but nothing really came of it until a riding school played it in an indoor arena.

Australians then took an interest in the game and finally developed and named the sport as we know it today.

It has become a fast developing sport around the globe and offers fast action entertainment for spectators.

At one of these tournaments and after the Saturday night dance that invariably went on to the early hours of the night, I staggered home and poured myself into bed.

Some hours later I woke with a thirst and went to the outhouse kitchen to get a glass of milk from the fridge. But entering through the door I fell over something big, warm and hairy.

On with the light, I discover one of Mike's prized bull taking up the whole kitchen space and was clearly not well.

A glass of milk to clear my head I thought, but that was not possible as he was leaning against the fridge door.

A couple of hours later the staff arrived to work and with difficulty, man handled it out of the kitchen but despite treatment it did not survive and Mike wanted to know what I was doing with a bull in my kitchen.

CHAPTER NINE
HORSES

Horses have been a big part of my life over the years and have given me so much pleasure. It is quite amazing how they can adapt to situations and I would watch on TV how the cowboy would get shot by the Indian warrior and the horse tumbles to the ground and think this was staged.

Maybe it isn't, but in the Grey Scouts I have seen horses do things that ordinarily one would not believe or certainly never usually risk asking them to do.

In the Grey Scouts we were given standard army Mercedes 7 tonne troop carrying trucks to ferry our horses around. The only change to the truck was that the seats were removed and the sides raised to prevent the horses from falling out.

Seven horses could fit in if they were pushed up with no poles in between and there was no loading ramp at the back but only poles to secure them in. Being 4x4 trucks they were also very high off the ground.

We would deploy sections going on patrol this way, often on very rough roads or going through the bush following paths or fence lines and the horses would have to jump out on arrival.

Being in a war zone, one could not loiter around for too long as this could present a target for easy picking at the most vulnerable time so it was important to complete the exercise as quickly as possible.

At the end of the patrol the trucks would arrive and it wasn't always convenient to find an embankment or anthill to assist with loading so the horses were trained to simply jump in. Remember, these trucks are high off the ground.

The last couple to load had it tough as there was little space left in the truck for them to land and so the best were kept to last.

They would jump and turn side on in one movement and collapse against the next horse to shunt them up and when the last one was in, he had the hardest task, the tail gate was shut and poles quickly slid into place before they settled.

Horses would become disorientated when they travelled great distances by truck from their static base and once off loaded, would generally go on a fourteen day patrol that would take them some distance from the off loading point.

If a contact occurred, the horses were abandoned and many of them would make their way back to that drop off point as the last familiar place and hang around to be collected. This was always the first point to search for these animals.

There have been some that turned up at the static base several weeks and sometimes months later, many kilometers away.

We operated in the Gonerezhou Game Reserve in the south east of the country for well over a year and based at Twiza that was a siding on the railway line to Villa Salazar on the border with Mozambique.

Being in a game reserve we were plagued by Lion.

Our standard practice when bivving up for the night on patrol, was to tie the horses to trees around the outside of our sleeping area.

Horses have very sensitive hearing and during the night, sentries would watch the horses ears if they had detected something. All the horses pointing in the same direction was a sure sign that something was out there.

But with the horses tied up they became easy prey for the Lions and because of the darkness one could not see what was going on in the racket that ensued.

It was then decided to tie the horses up in the inner circle and we would sleep around the outer edge to protect them. But this didn't work either.

The Lions simply slipped past us and one could not see if you were about to get trampled on by stampeding horses that had broken their ropes.

One little grey of about 14.3 hands high had a Lion on its back and managed to buck and kick the Lion off and lived to tell the tail. It suffered rake marks all down its sides.

There was a time that big cattle ranches in the midlands had horses that for some reason were released on the ranch and over many years bred up into herds of wild horses;

Devuli Ranch comes to mind as having the biggest herds. One could buy these horses by the cattle truck load and after rounding them up, herd them into RMS cattle trucks, take them home and break them in for resale.

Generally they were not a good quality of horse having been inbred over generations but there was a market for them as cattle ponies.

I tried it, only I didn't buy mine from Devuli but from Rob Rooken-Smith who ranched at Lalapanzi, a chrome mining area on the Dyke in the midlands.

There was fuel rationing at the time and as I couldn't raise enough fuel coupons I decided to use the railways to ferry them to Lochinvar siding in Salisbury.

The herd I selected from had a number of Stallions and I was not interested in them so they were singled out and I got my mares and one with a young colt.

Offloading them from the rail wagon into the cattle crush at Lochinvar I was able to put halters on them and then tied them in pairs to herd them over the vlei to my rented property in Tynwold, a suburb of Salisbury.

Being tied together like this prevented them from bolting as they could seldom coordinate an escape plan together. I would head them in the right direction using my Polocrosse horse to ride them off on the right line. It was an interesting exercise but they all arrived safely and put into stables.

If one intended to make money out of them then they had to be handled and saddle broken quickly before they ate all the profits in food.

I started by approaching them in the stable at night by blinding them with a torch and slowly putting my hand near their nostril to smell me. This would progress until the animal trusted me enough for me to touch it and they would not come out of their stable until I could handle it without it being scared.

The next exercise was to bring it out and familiarize it with the bridle and eventually the saddle.

Usually, at this stage it was fine until the girth was tightened and away it would go bucking for all its worth to get rid of the saddle. But we always had it at the end of a long rope and let it buck until it realized it was not going to lose the saddle.

At this point I would put the stirrups on and mount and away it would go again. But the fire would have gone out of it and it wouldn't be long before it accepted that it could not get rid of its burden.

The trick here was not to fall off as it would then get the idea that it can be done and a lot of time wasted to start over.

I turned all of them over very quickly except one black mare that resembled Celia's Gypsy from the farm in Melsetter and I called her that.

She took forever to gain my trust and was always very skittish as well as being pretty accurate with her legs, kicking both backwards and forward.

I failed to get her to point of sale as she trusted me but only me. She was a lost cause and I still had her when I moved onto the farm in the Mazoe Valley below Christian Bank where I worked for the Fishers.

One day she got thoroughly tangled up in a mass of barbed wire and was on her side thrashing away in panic and making her situation worse.

I approached her with trepidation knowing how well she kicks and in that panic mode I did not know what she would do.

I was therefore overwhelmed with feeling when she recognized me and lay perfectly still as I cut away the wire and in some places precariously vulnerable.

But Gypsy had to go. Before a prospective buyer arrived I would put an hour of work into her so that she would behave and not give that rude snort as the buyer approached, but she always succeeded in putting the buyer off.

With my last buyer I put in extra time with her, but she arrived and said she only wanted her as a brood mare to breed from and didn't need to ride her.

What a relief. This person was Mrs. Worthington from Charter Estates, a big cattle and crop farm south of Salisbury and Gypsy left for a comfortable life of breeding.

I had never owned my own horse, always riding one of Sheila Barry's until I arrived in Salisbury and started working for the Sugar Refineries.

My first pay cheque went on a horse that I bought from June Brink just out of town and on the Bulawayo road.

He was an ex race horse and not in good condition and as such was affordable to me.

He came with a halter and I had sufficient funds to buy a basic bridle but not enough for a saddle. His name was Happy Hero.

His condition, I think, was from drug abuse from his racing days and he was for ever getting sick with colic that for the first few months I couldn't ride him.

Dr Everard Cock of Cock and Thoroughgood vetinary surgery...... what parent would be so cruel as to give their son a name like that, was constantly visiting him and running up a huge vet bill that I would have to borrow money off my father to meet.

I had rented a stable in the Show Grounds amongst about six other people and we formed a great little community of friends that would share in each other's problems, have evening braai's and generally do everything together.

Hero medically was coming right but struggled to gain condition, none the less I was able to ride him.

But he was a dreadful rearer and would run backwards then rear up and flip over on his back in one quick movement. He also had the nasty habit of running back wards into trees or stationary cars before doing his rear.

Usually a horse will rear out of shear naughtiness and will only rear to the height before he loses control of his balance as he too will want to preserve himself from injury and should he come over, will try to fall on his side.

A good lesson for a horse like this is to actually pull him over and give him a fright that hopefully he will have second thought of doing it again, but with Hero it was like a panic thing that he would keep repeating.

I was due to do my National Service and Sheila Barry offered to look after him for the duration of my nine months training.

I put him on the train with all his kit to head for Umtali and as I had no groom, went with him.

Being the only horse in the cattle wagon I secured him in as best I could with ropes and poles as the railways insisted that the doors were left open when humans travelled in the wagon, I guess in case of an accident.

He was fine until the shunting started to couple up all the wagons and then he went ballistic.

It was a very worrying time especially as we were finally coupled up behind the diesel engine and then spent hours in the main station for passengers to board the coaches behind us.

Hero wanted to get out of that wagon at all cost and I just could not calm him down. This persisted all the way down to Umtali on this over night train and with no sleep; I was physically exhausted when I got him out at the Umtali Main Station. I rode him to the farm some twelve miles away.

Sheila did wonders for this horse. When I completed my national service I went down to collect him and could hardly recognize him he had put on so much weight with a shining coat that he looked quite handsome.

Hero had a very good jump in him when he put his mind to it so I entered the Salisbury Agricultural Show's D grade jumping event.

My name was called up on the loud speaker as the next competitor and I had to ride through the entrance gate in the castle wall and into the arena to commence jumping the course.

Hero took exception to the Castle wall gate and started his running backwards and rearing.

People came to my assistance, hanging on to his head whilst others tried to shoo him forward.

My name came up three times on the intercom before they belled me out as not turning up and I ended my career as a show jumper from that moment onwards. Oh for the love of one's first horse.

An attractive young lady turned up at the stables in the show grounds, dressed up like mother

Christmas in her red coat, boots and hood with fluffy white trimmings that I had a double take.

She introduced herself then promptly burst into tears and poured out her woes.

She has a pony, she tells me, and cannot afford to keep it. She needs the money and please would I buy it off her.

I didn't actually need another horse but to appease her I went along to see it.

It was a runt thoroughbred mare originating from the Karroo in South Africa and stood 14.2 hands high. A bit small for me and under conditioned but the lady pulled on my heart strings and I bought it.

The mare was called Gay Marina and was one of my best buys. Her heart was bigger than her body and she gave me so much pleasure over the years, being prepared to do anything I asked of her.

Farming in Norton, I would go shooting Franklin in the evenings as they dug up and ate the newly planted maize seeds.

She would stand stock still as I fired off her back with a shot gun. Then on the weekends play a good game of Polocrosse on her at the Borrowdale Country Club in Salisbury.

I eventually sold her on to a youngster named Graeme Wilkins who showed great potential in Polocrosse and in itself rewarded me for parting with a good friend.

Many years later, in 1992, I managed the Zimbabwean Test match squads to South Africa and discovered Graeme had made the Springbok South African side.

Reading the personal profiles of the players, Graeme wrote how he started his Polocrosse career on Gay Marina, a pony he loved and how she put him into top level Polocrosse. I was touched.

I was at a Gymkana at the Borrowdale Club and took along a new trainee groom who had no idea how to ride.

At the end of the day there was a groom's race that was the length of the Polocrosse field and my guy wanted to enter. Because Gay Marina was safe I let him do so.

He climbed up on her back and took on that pose of a baby monkey clinging on to its mother with his legs scrunched up high and his body spread across her back and up her neck.

The starter's orders went and Marina took off without instruction from the lump on her back.

Into the lead she went but by now the groom was losing contact with the horse apart from the mane which he clung to in desperation whilst the rest of his body started flailing in the slip stream.

Marina won the race but didn't stop at the finish; instead she disappeared down the embankment that led to the stables at the far side of the field. There I found her with one ecstatic groom still clinging on to her mane.

CHAPTER TEN
HOUSE ATTACK.

The war was escalating, land mines and farm attacks were taking their toll on farmers on the front lines and those bordering the communal areas. The guerrillas would strike at night before melting away amongst the peasant population.

These peasant folk were caught between a rock and a hard place and were forced to feed and hide the guerillas or face serious reprisals by having villages destroyed, face dismembership rituals or succumb to public executions.

The Rhodesian forces on follow up would require information that sometimes required rough handling to get this intelligence expeditially but their tactics could never match the ruthless torture of the aptly named Terrorist. This tended to result in disinformation or little too late from nervous peasants.

Village children were formed into spies called 'Mujiba's' who would report to the guerillas on security force movements and on their parents and families to root out anyone disloyal to their cause or identify 'sell outs'.

Recruiting of able bodied males and females were undertaken, often by force, and sent off to neighbouring countries for training and whole schools and mission stations would be rounded up and taken across the border for 'further education'.

Farmers on these borders had it rough. If not being attacked in their homes they would be on the constant look out for land mines, a very effective demoralizer, or have their crops destroyed, livestock slaughtered or stolen or labour abducted.

A number of these farmers had reached their threshold and left their farms. The Rhodesian Government could ill afford to have these farms abandoned as, by their vacancy, would add to the security problem.

So through the government land bank, the Agricultural Finance Corporation, 100% loans were offered to young aspiring farmers to occupy and work these farms.

Three farms became available in the Horseshoe Block and I decided to take the plunge and apply.

I chose Bonheim Farm, a very hot farm in the furthest north and on the edge of the escarpment. The owner had had enough and was leaving the country and wanted to sell it lock stock.

The AFC scheme was a 'Tennant Farmer Scheme' but I figured I was not prepared to go to these lengths of risk if at the end of the war I didn't get to own the farm and as it was such a hot farm, an exception was made in my case and I was provided a 20 year loan to purchase the farm outright.

Much to an unhappy Mike I left, very excited to move onto my own farm. The first night, sleeping in this large bedroom on suite with mattress on the floor and my army FN Rifle complete with webbing and with loaded magazines beside my bed, I was at the ready. I went to sleep in that dreamy feeling of excitement of being a land owner.

I do not sleep in bed clothes but like to sleep as nature intended. Sometime in the middle of the night I was woken to a racket of automatic gun fire and explosions of rockets going over the roof of the house.

This is 'it' I thought, the real thing. Time to get up and fight a war but I cannot do this naked so had to get dressed first. On with my pants but they were inside out so removed them and reversed them.

They were still inside out so I sat on the mattress and tried to figure out what was going on. One leg was inside out but the other was not and I was just switching them over every time I inverted them.

Having got myself ready for battle I ran

down the passageway and hit the red handle of the Agric Alert that all farmers had to link them to the Police Station.

A reaction unit would be on its way. But then, I thought, what do I do now. Get out of the house I reasoned and join up with the unit of 4 guys known as Guard Force that the government provided for security.

Going out the back entrance of the house yard that leads to the barns, I discover that it is not only me under attack but also the guard force in their building behind the farm store. Beyond that I could see flames coming from the farm workers compound.

I went back into the house and sat it out knowing that the reaction stick would not be long.

The main road into the Zambezi valley from Sipolilo divided my farm and went past the barn complex. It was narrow tar up to my neighbours where it became gravel and this was frequently mined as it was a well used road and security force convoys used it to access the valley.

Andy Lange, the Member in charge, now informs me on the Agric Alert that the reaction stick is at Camperdown at the end of the tar and as a precaution was walking in.

So this will take longer I thought but then the attack broke off and that haunting silence ensued after the racket.

The next morning I surveyed the damage. Apart from a few bullet holes in the outside walls of the house, everything had passed harmlessly over the top.

The guard force building on the other hand had nearly been flattened by RPG rocket fire; how they survived the attack can only be put down to good luck and a natural burying instinct.

The compound was empty of humanity and apart from a few huts; the rest were burnt to the ground.

The labour and their families had been rounded up and driven with sticks into the reserve next door. Some, including children, had broken arms and legs from the beatings.

I stood on the high ground surveying the devastation in that early morning calm that defies belief that this took place. The smoke still hung low as I felt the first feeling of panic that this is no game, that lives are involved and how was I to continue now that I had hocked myself to the limit. There was no turning back and I couldn't see a way forward.

Preoccupied in these depressing thoughts, I noticed a door open from one of the few un burnt huts and a young mute lad that I had employed as a tobacco nurseryman, emerge with a look of absolute horror at the devastation all around him.

He had been unaware of all that had happened that night and had slept through it all. He took off from there and I have never seen or heard anything of him since.

The community rallied and tractors and trailers turned up with labour, poles, thatch and all the building materials needed to build me a new compound on the other side of the main road and close to the barns. A security fence was erected and a guard house in the compound built to protect the workers and their families.

Arthur Beamish, my neighbour on Camperdown was the organizer behind this and achieved this in three days. Sadly, the next day he was killed in his lands by guerillas at lunch time whilst he was ridging his tobacco lands. The reality of all this sunk home to me and from then on I lived on my nerves.

Everything had been repaired and security systems put in place but I had no labour to farm with. Those that returned from the reserve disappeared and I could not recruit new labour after this had happened.

Andy Lang gave me prisoners from his jail and my brother Digby came to help me and to protect my back whilst I drove the tractor and prepared my ridges for tobacco planting.

The prisoners were hopeless, no desire to work and would disappear at the slightest opportunity when your eyes were not on them. Andy took them back, well those that hadn't escaped.

Driving back from the lands one day I was flagged down by an African who enquired about a job. I could have given him a hug and a kiss at this remarkable opportunity. "Can you drive a tractor" I said. "Oh yes" he lied. "Jump on let's see" I replied in hope.

He had no idea at all, but that was a minor detail, he was going to be my driver I determined. His name was Mabuross, the way shonas say Mulberries, and I taught him to drive and had him for many years as my head driver.

Gail, Arthurs wife was paid out by insurance and asked me if I would continue with Arthur's tobacco on the other side of my boundary.

By now I had managed to recruit a labour force. Reaping this tobacco, my labour would fly through it, constantly looking over their shoulders.

On a couple of occasions a contact would take place not far into the reserve and my tractors would fly out of there at speeds that had the trailer flailing behind, spewing tobacco everywhere and sometimes overturning.

The drivers would disappear out of there so fast without any consideration for the labour who would attempt to run after the tractor screaming for it to wait.

On one occasion, going to the lands on my motor bike, I saw black movement in the long grass up ahead. Sure I was running into an ambush, I shot off into the bush diving off the bike for cover as I did. Nothing happened, my heart racing, and then a turkey buzzard took off in a lazy mocking flight.

We had a few more attacks, less severe but none the less had a bad morale effect on us all. Everyone was tense, locked down by three in the afternoon to face yet another sleepless night of anxiety only to rise at six, weary to face the next day's work. None of which could start until the guard force had searched the roads for land mines.

I would bath straight after work at three and it would always be a quick one with my rifle and kit close to hand as I felt terribly vulnerable. For the rest of the time I would be fully clothed and ready.

Later, when the nerves where at its rawest, I would sit in the small toilet cubicle down the passage as the safest place to be until 3 in the morning when I figured an attack unlikely.

My nerves were so tuned for sound that every expansion or contraction of the steel roof would not allow me to relax for a minute.

The labour too were going through the same emotions. An attack was preferable to the wait. Adrenalin would carry you through and it would all be over within half an hour. The relief after it all meant a reasonable sleep.

I was standing in the middle of a land watching my tractor harrowing. The weather had been building up and out of the blue came a huge lighting strike followed by a big thunder clap.

Instinctively, I hit the ground then looked up to find my tractor still harrowing but minus a driver. He had jumped off and sped to the bush for cover. The nerves were telling.

We all felt that our domestic staff were the most vulnerable and could be used to get access to you so I turned my office in the court yard into accommodation for William my cook and his family.

He had come to me early in the evening asking me to radio up the guard force to escort him to the compound and get a midwife as his wife was about to deliver.

The attack started while William was in the compound but this time they used mortars.

The AK firing sounded distant and I was sure this attack was a decoy to ambush the reaction stick so advised Andy not to send them in but wait at Camperdown.

The mortars were falling around the barn complex but were ineffective except one that blew the horse paddock fence. Soon the reaction stick at Camperdown radioed saying my horses had galloped past up the road.

The usual deathly quiet after it was all over and then the sounds of a baby cry. Poor girl had given birth in the office on her own. The next morning William decided to name his new daughter 'Mortar Bomb'.

A Msasa tree had been knocked over and slightly damaged the office roof and no doubt had given the final impetus to push. But it had pulled the telephone line down and snapped the flex leading to the house.

My mechanic, Takesure, was a very gullible character and I could never resist the opportunity to pull a prank on him.

This opportunity came. I asked him to repair the roof but whilst up there to join the broken line. First, I said, I want to check if the phone is working so hold the two wires coming from the house, and I will go in and say "hallo Takesure" into the receiver and you tell me if you hear me.

Off I went to the old fashioned crank handle set and gave the handle a turn. A shriek was heard and on going out I enquired if he heard me. "No no" he said "but the wires bite me" still holding onto the wires and with a confused look on his face.

I had been correct. I paced the distance to their firing point and it was a thousand yards. Somehow they had managed to plot this. From this point you could not see the buildings and the AK gooks had fun shooting up the trees right in front of them.

One AK was abandoned, the barrel had exploded and I assume he forgot to take out whatever he used to cover the barrel with to keep it clean or it was choked with mud. We were lucky at their general lack of combat skills.

Takesure would not sleep in the compound. He preferred the safety of the workshop and slept in the vehicle inspection pit. He would remark in the morning how he would watch the stars coming through the iron roof, referring to the tracer rounds.

I had met a very pretty girl called Sue Johnson on one of my infrequent shopping trips to Salisbury.

She worked for Rhonat, my insurance company and together with a friend I knew called Val Mason from Rhodesdale, we persuaded Sue to go out for lunch with me and a very short relationship started.

Being on the farm on my own was very lonely and especially as there was no more social life for me. No one would visit me on the farm, Alex tried once and was ambushed on his way home, but my friend Ian Brown would often risk it and stay for supper and over night with me. Those were golden moments.

I needed companionship and I wanted to marry Sue so I popped the question and she accepted.

By now Andy Lang had given me two Police Reservists, known as bright lights to live with me for my protection. These guys were on call up and usually came from Sinoia and were a welcome comfort. I figured it would be ok to bring a new bride home.

I had to ask permission from Andy if I was to be off the farm over night but on this occasion I hadn't and instead took Sue off to Kariba for the weekend to celebrate our engagement.

Whilst at Kariba, the 'gooks' brought in people from the reserve and with their scotch carts, reaped a whole land of maize over night.

I was in serious trouble with Andy on my return and he removed my bright lights as they were there for my protection not the farm.

We planned our wedding date and arranged for the army chaplain to marry us and then planned a honeymoon to Durban in South Africa. I was very excited about the prospect and to have time away from the farm.

The night before I was to come into town for our wedding, I had another attack. This time an RPG 7 rocket glanced off a Msasa branch and exploded through the small passage toilet, the one I usually sit in thinking it was the safest place.

I was running down the passage at the time and can remember the intense heat of it as well as being showered with flying pieces of brick. Every window in the house was blown out and the roof lifted and damaged.

My neighbours and friends, Dick and Sue Marr came around in the morning and told me to get in the car and go and get married. They would sort out the mess. But driving into town I now had serious reservations about bringing Sue out to the farm.

I met Sue and her mother for tea at the George Hotel and told her the wedding was off. Mortified, she would not have it and even her mother supported her decision. I thought, you crazy woman, you have no idea what it is like, but deep down I was happy at that.

She then took me off to Dr Zinn to have the pieces of brick and glass removed from my back and legs and the marriage ceremony took place at the Park Lane hotel.

My dear farmer friends brought in bales of

tobacco scrap and used it in place of confetti so there was no matrimonial sex that night as we were both self absorbed in scratching all night.

Honey moon was a week at the Four Seasons Hotel in Durban and was rather disastrous. Sue had second thoughts about married life and we started on the wrong foot.

Friends had joined us on honey moon and that gave us a bit of distraction. Nev and Edie Pierce were also staying in the same hotel and I would ask Nev miserably, "Why did you not warn me married life is like this?" and Sue would be asking Edie the same thing.

Sue had a 3 year old son Roger from a previous marriage. Not having the opportunity to be Roger's mother for the past three years had affected Sue and she became obsessed with making up for it. Shopping centered on Roger and I made the mistake of wasting money buying a watch from an Indian street seller.

We were sitting on the open veranda having tea with the Pearce's when I was invited to buy this watch. The Indian chap was wearing a great coat and he opened the front of his coat to display rows of watches.

I went down to see and selected a gold watch that had a popular maker's name. I thought I had a bargain but Nev chinked the strap and said no way was it gold. He also pointed out the missing letter in the name saying "this is a fake and you have been had!"

This was a bad move in Sue's eyes and I had to redeem myself so took off down the street to find this chap. I soon found him on a street corner and asked "are you the chap that sold me this watch?" "No, no, no!" he replied in that Indian accent. "I don't sell watches" he lied. "Oh, that's a pity" I said "I was hoping to buy another one". On that he opened his coat revealing all the watches saying "I am sure we can find something here!"

But despite all my efforts I could not get him to refund me and ended up giving it to William on our return where it promptly packed up.

We arrived back from honeymoon to the farm and walked into a transformed house. Dick and Sue had replaced all the corrugated iron roof sheeting, fixed the windows and bricked up the hole in the wall.

On the coffee table in the lounge was a huge bouquet of flowers with a note that said 'Welcome Home'. How privileged we are to have such wonderful people as friends.

The pantry was the only room not cleaned out as it had been locked but gave Sue the idea of what the house was like with all the dust and rubble still in there.

She cleaned it out including my prized

stocks of tinned food that I had inherited and now showing signs of rust.

The house was transformed in another way, the way that women do to turn a bachelor pad into a cozy nest that becomes their domain.

William and I looked at each other knowingly, I secretly liked the idea but William's days as a bachelor cook were over. Gone were the days of being dropped off at the supermarket and having the field of choice and gone were the days that he made the decisions of what to eat and how to keep house.

Not only was I know married but had an instant family to boot. It was a big learning curve for me especially as I was not that great with little kids, but I put my mind to my new role and enjoyed it.

I built a bunker in the house with sand bags and made it Roger's bedroom. Sue fancied it up with decorations.

But I was very unsettled with Sue's attitude towards the war. It was all a game and exciting to be a part of it, in some ways much like I had been on that first night's attack and it worried me intensely. I went over procedures with her in the event of an attack but she glossed over it.

We were in bed, Sue curled up in that foetal position, happy as a kettle on the boil snoring away as I lay awake with nerves on edge.

The instant the first rounds left the AK's I sprung into action as a compressed spring suddenly released. I gave Sue such a hard kick up the butt with my leg that she went flying across the fitted carpet floor, still semi asleep but now arms flailing in panic. Dragged her into the bunker and then got an earful for frightening her like that and complaining bitterly about her carpet burns on her knees.

CHAPTER ELEVEN
CEASE FIRE.

The Lancaster house conference had pulled together some sort of an agreement amongst all the leaders and an end to the war was imminent.

Rhodesia was to return to its pre UDI status as a colony under the British Government and Lord Soames was to be the Governor.

Rhodesian forces were confined to barracks except those required to maintain law and order and the Nationalist's guerillas were to hand themselves in to designated collection points under the control of an international monitoring force.

All of this would then lead up to the first one man one vote elections.

I was happy the war was coming to an end, I had had enough, it played on my nerves and I was not able to farm properly.

But nobody trusted the nationalists especially Zanu led by Robert Mugabe who covered the greater part of the country.

He was ruthless and cunning and would not deviate from his ambition of total power. No matter what he said publically, he stuck to his agenda.

He armed non combatants and sent them into the collection points, made up the numbers and who could argue what forces he really had. His combatants he kept back to use for the upcoming elections.

No one wanted the war to continue, the country was war weary and just wanted to get on with life and that was Mugabe's keystone for his campaign.

He still had his forces and the message was 'vote for me if you want the war to stop'. He then enforced this with brutal intimidation and all night political rallies called Pungwe's.

Our security chiefs warned Soames of this development but as with the British government, he turned a blind eye and wanted to get it over with.

The result was obvious, an over whelming victory to Mugabe who became the first black Prime Minister of Zimbabwe.

The people had voted for no war.

I had a collection point on my boundary and was situated under a hill on the very edge of the escarpment that commanded a magnificent view over the Zambezi valley.

For this reason, the Police ran a radio relay station known as Foxtrot Alfa and manned 24 hours by police reservists. It was important that it continued operating but the guerillas in the camp at its base were not happy and it buzzed with volatility like a nest of wasps.

This collection point was run by a British military unit with a Captain in charge and I befriended them and had them over every night for a hot meal and a bath.

Over a beer, the Captain would tell me of his encounters that occurred that day and one was when a particularly aggressive guerrilla commander demanded that Foxtrot Alfa be disbanded.

He emphasized his point by sticking the barrel of his AK up the Captains nose, but being all British he defused the situation by saying "Now, now old boy, this is simply not the way we British do things. Let us sit down like gentlemen and discuss this matter over a cup of tea!" He was very proud of this.

The Captain had sent a section down the escarpment road to encourage known gooks too insecure to come into the collection point. Unfortunately they hit a land mine near Mahuwe at the bottom of the escarpment.

These British Army Land Rovers were magnificent and I wanted one being a Land Rover enthusiast.

Over dinner I asked the Captain about the damage that had happened to it and he assured me it was not that bad. "Can I have it?" I said hopefully. "Sure" he replied, "but you will have to collect it yourself as we are abandoning it there."

I organized a tractor and a big enough trailer and together with my labour we were going down, me driving, to manhandle this wreck on board.

As we were about to leave, a Police Nissan Patrol comes flying into the yard. Andy Lange had wind of my venture somehow and he was spitting mad. "You set one foot on that road and I will lock you up and throw the keys away!" he huffed. "If anything happened to these guys" pointing to my labour "and they get killed, you will be up for murder!"

He had a point and I lost my Land Rover.

It was particularly unsettling for Sue and I to see lines of these 'comrades' walking past our house fully armed as they moved to the collection point. But more so when two very drunk gooks decided to walk into our house.

At the time, I had the area manager Peter de la Harpe from the AFC as well as the local inspector doing a tour of the district and they were in the lounge where Sue was giving them tea.

Paul Savory, who was now working for me,

came running into the kitchen white faced and before he could get the words out to warn me, these two drunks were in the kitchen.

It is one thing to have to defuse a situation with a sober gook but quite another with a drunk one wielding his AK and with stick grenades popping out of his pockets.

They wanted to come in they said. "You are not welcome" I replied. "Why, we have won the war, this is a black country now and you are being racist!" they slurred. "No one is welcome in my house carrying weapons" I said, and believe it or not, they accepted that point and staggered out.

Peter and his inspector sat in their chairs gob smacked. "Bring the car around" says Peter to his inspector after he found his voice "we are going". "But surely you want to see the crops" I said knowing full well they were not hanging around for anything. "Another time" he says as they disappeared around the corner.

At a Coffee field day in Banket sometime later, I was singled out to meet the AFC delegation that Peter led and the 'war story' was repeated with a little gloss.

At the time I was the AFC's blue eyed boy and could do no wrong in Peter's eyes. The war was over and I could farm better resulting in being a finalist in the national Maize Grower of the Year competition.

I wanted to reduce my risk in dry land farming and introduce irrigation to apply water little but often to penetrate the crusty soils I had. Heavy rainfalls tended to run off.

I spoke to my advisor and accountant Peter Thomas about a possible dam site that was between me and the neighbouring farm that would irrigate the blocks of land on both farms next to each other. It meant buying that farm to get the benefit of the scheme.

Peter Thomas brought a delegation out to the farm that included a dam engineer and soil specialist and the site was surveyed.

Over lunch the scheme was discussed and they all went back to do their respective parts of the project including crop rotations. Peter de la Harpe was on board and pledged AFC assistance.

I was advised to buy Chiringi, the farm next door for cash and use it as extra collateral to borrow for the irrigation scheme and dam construction. The next step of design commenced.

I was summoned to the AFC Head Quarters in Harare and walked into the office expecting to see Peter. Instead I was confronted by a newspaper with legs under it resting on the table.

"I am Chris Pocock", I said "you wanted to see me, where is Peter?"

"I know who you are" he replied without putting the paper down, "I have replaced Peter and you are not getting that loan for the project!"

He then put the paper down, lent forward across the table and glared saying he will not put a mill stone around my neck as I was doing well enough dry land. End of story.

Peter had left to emigrate to South Africa.

That was the beginning of the end for me. I now had two dry land farms, huge commitments to pay for the failed project and the following three consecutive droughts brought my farming to an end.

I fell out with the AFC as I refused to give them Chiringi as collateral and instead used it with a Commercial bank to raise money to crop.

I was a member of the Farmers Cooperative and it was useful in getting certain inputs on stop order. I went in to see the usual guy I had been seeing and he tells me he had been superseded and that I should see 'God'.

'God was in the next office and on going in I was confronted yet again by a newspaper with legs that had familiar shoes.

The man had a short life with the AFC and had now taken over the credit department of the Farmers Coop. I came out empty handed.

Back to Takesure, my mechanic.

Not only was he gullible but quite a sensitive lad. Forever having domestic issues, he tried a few times to commit suicide but always failed. Either it was poisoning from some tobacco chemical he had stolen or on one occasion, he tried hanging himself from a tree. Either way he was just not good at it.

We were working on a planter one morning and his wife walked up and placed his crawling child at his feet and walked away. The baby crawled after her screaming blue murder and she simply picked it up and replaced it at his feet again.

I asked her what she thought she was doing and she replied that she was taking her belongings and going back to her parents. "The baby is his and I am leaving him!" she said determinedly.

Takesure stood there with his eyes firmly fixed on me as if to say, give me the order and I will fix her. But instead I said, "Takesure, sort your problems out, we have work to do!"

He chased after her and she ran across the road to the cattle loading ramp where she had all her kit waiting for the bus to take her down to the valley. On getting there, she picked up an enamel pot and beat seven colours of shit out of him, so badly that I had to intervene and rush him off to the clinic for stitches.

Having got that little dispute out of the way, she returned home to him and lived happily ever after, well, until the next one came along.

Driving down the valley with Takesure in my Landy, I mentioned to him how rough the roads are and that it would be better to have a plane and fly.

He put on his thoughtful look and engaged in serious conversation with me suggesting that that would be a good idea.

"Ah" I said, "but that will be expensive. You know you can get these planes that look like a bicycle. It is just a pipe frame with a seat and a lawn mower engine behind with plastic sheeting for wings. Very cheap," I said as his thoughtful expression changed slightly to alarm.

"But what if the engine fails, just like the lawn mower at the house, it is always failing and you will fall from heaven and die!"

"No it won't happen" I said reassuringly "because there is another seat behind me for you to sit in and we can make a place for your tool box and when the engine dies, you can fix it. No it will be quite safe like that?" I said as I watched his face turn to panic.

After a long silence of deep thought he said "I am putting in my notice and I want to leave at the end of this month. I am too young and I have not made enough children to die now."

"Come now" I replied "you are always trying to commit suicide, at least this way you won't fail."

"That is another matter" he spluttered out "You are crazy and I don't want to die with you!" We rattled on for the rest of the journey in silence.

CHAPTER TWELVE
FAMILY

We decided that I should adopt Roger.

It was quite a performance requiring approval of his blood father, filling out documents with the Ministry of Welfare who then sent out a lady to inspect the home he is living in and to interview me if I should be a suitable father.

Something I found strange as I would have a family of my own in time. Would they say I was not suitable to breed?

Sue was riding on her nerves as we showed her around and then finally to the dining room table for the final interrogation.

Pointed questions were asked as to how I would deal with certain situations and one dealt with a disciplinary requirement. What would I do was the question. "Oh" I said with a straight face "tie him to a tree and whip him severely".

"You are joking!" she exclaimed in horror.

"Yes" I said still with a dead pan face.

It broke the ice and she relaxed her official demeanor and passed me. Sue climbed back from under the table.

But Roger was not an easy child, he showed little emotion and for a while I think resented leaving Granny and Granddad who had basically been his parents as Sue had to work all day.

One day whilst in the bath, Sue marched Roger in and instructed me to give Roger a hiding for something serious he had done and walked out leaving Roger staring at the wall. Why do mothers do this I thought?

I got to the bottom of the story, and pointed out why he was about to get a hiding. In the meantime, pull your pants down, bend over and think about what you did wrong, while I finish bathing.

I slipped out of the bathroom very quietly and left him there, eye's screwed up in anticipation. After a while I stood in the door way and said "Why are you bending over with your pants down!"

He leapt up in surprise pulling up his pants and said "I am waiting for a hiding!"

"Don't do that again!" I replied with an air of satisfied authority.

I found it difficult to deal with this no emotion. I wanted to win him over but couldn't gauge my success. I would ask, do you want to ride on the tractor. "If you want" he would say without expression and I would feel like putting a squib up his ass.

I took him in my Land Rover to a new land we were stumping. There were a lot of thorns so advised him to stay in the Land Rover and I would be back soon. I didn't. I got carried away with the stumping.

Soon Roger hobbled his way to me and said "Dad, I have been sick."

"What!" I freaked. "In my Land Rover! Let's go and see."

I had visions of child puke over my seat but when I got there I could see no trace of this offensive bile. I even looked in the hole where the gear shift comes through and only saw wholesome oil mixed dust. "So where is this sick?" I ask.

"I am sick and tired of waiting" he said logically. What can you do but laugh.

Back to the end of the war, Roger developed a stomach pain at some late hour in the night. It was not possible to get him to a doctor with the risk of landmines and ambush.

The next morning we took him in to hospital and he had had a burst appendix that involved an operation to remove some of his intestines.

I felt bad and bought an expensive remote control Mercedes car to cheer him up. He accepted it without emotion and on the next visit I discovered that he had smashed it. I was mortified;

I wanted to play with it.

I wanted a child of my own but figured that if we had a son, I would run the risk of favoritism and so it had to be a girl.

I willed a girl and it bothered Sue, "What if it is a boy?" she would say. "I know it is a girl!" and I was confident.

But we had to pick names for both sex. Sue wanted Emma for a girl and I did not like it so I went for the extreme and suggested Zoe, "Short for Mazoe if you like."

"I am not having my daughter called by that name!" she huffed and had the full support of the family and friends.

But it allowed for a compromise and we settled on Tara Anne, both names that had special meaning.

Sue was game, being a townie. We had friends out for the weekend and the four of us went on the tractor and trailer to Foxtrot Alfa to take in the scenery of the valley below. Being pregnant, I put her in a deck chair on the trailer.

After a hot and dusty ride over a corrugated road we arrived at the summit to find Sue had transformed from white to a respectable brown with very large eyes where her sunglasses had shielded the dust.

Tara arrived in the world when I was playing Polocrosse against South Africa at Thorn Park. This would be the last time we played South Africa for twelve years as they were now enemies of our new government.

I made it on time to see Tara arrive into the world at the end of a pair of forceps. I thought my daughter would be beautiful but she wasn't, she was scrunched up, distorted and noisy. Her beauty only came later.

But none the less, I was over the moon and rushed off to the registry office to register her birth.

In my excitement I forgot to fill in her proper surname. We have a double barrel surname in Innes - Pocock but do not use it and I omitted the Innes on her birth certificate that has peeved Tara ever since. "It won't matter" I said "You will get married one day".

Sue had recruited an experienced nanny to look after Tara and I found her arrogant. She could speak good English and it worked for Sue. But I couldn't take it much longer and fired her.

Sue was miffed and we had a fight. "Don't worry" I said "I will get you someone better". So I went into the grading shed and selected a widowed girl named Alice.

Alice was polite, a little shy but always enthusiastic whatever she did, only she could not speak a word of English. "How am I going to communicate with her?" Sue moaned.

"Just learn shona" I said taking my life in my hands. She didn't need to, after a period of comical gesticulation Alice soon learnt English and threw herself into the job and remained with my kid's right through to adulthood and became part of the family.

Tara was artistic from an early age. She would take this yellow smelly goo from her nappy and paint patterns on the wall and I would have to study her very carefully before I could pick her up for a cuddle.

I am afraid I am not one of those fathers that can share in baby maintenance. Nappy changing was definitely beyond me although I did make an attempt once when my son Nicholas joined us.

Folding the nappy to the right size was higher grade but trying to fit it onto a tiny wriggling piece of humanity was a test of my ability. Having done it and on picking him up, it all fell off onto the floor.

Sue was a member of a bridge club run by Mary Leared and on this particular day she was going to be away over lunch time. Alice too would be off and frankly I felt panicky.

This was a huge responsibility for two hours and I prayed that Tara would be considerate and not share her nappy source.

For an hour and three quarters we played happily in the dining room and I forgot that these nasty events can take place until I picked up her plastic bunch of keys.

They were covered in a yellow substance and now on my hands. I looked towards the suspicious area of her nappy and sure enough it was being extruded at an alarming rate.

I froze; I couldn't touch anything or leave her alone as I begged her not to move and spread it.

I had to wait for Alice but she was now five minutes late so I yelled for her hoping someone would hear.

Someone did, it was Takesure my mechanic who came running as though something seriously dramatic had happened. It had and he rushed off to find Alice who arrived looking terribly concerned thinking the worst, then took in the scene and cracked up laughing.

We decided to move house and settle on Chiringi. I hired Charlie Page to manage Bonheim and he took over that house.

Chiringi was peaceful being off the main road and had a thatched house that we liked.

Sue's parents, living in Greendale, Harare, had inherited a stray dog that was a cross between a poodle and a fox terrier having the typical long curly hair.

Meredith, Sue's mother had a Corgi and it objected to the new lodger now named Jimmy so she asked if we could take him to the farm. I was not keen on the dog but obliged and Jimmy moved in with us.

Walking in the lands on Bonheim with Charlie, I remarked, "Look at this stupid dog" as he staggered drunkenly in front of us. The heat had got on top of him and being unfit he battled to coordinate his legs in any meaningful way but I liked his guts not to give up. We became those firm friends that one recalls in a lifetime.

Following me behind the motorbike or horse he became super fit and had quite a turn of speed, so much so that at the Horseshoe club one Saturday night I felt brave enough to brag about it to Mary and Nick Leared saying there was no dog to beat him.

"Not so" says Mary indignantly, "My Schipperke is faster" and so the challenge was on.

The venue was set at the club for the following Saturday and the community turned out in numbers. A tote was established and betting began. A third dog entered the race and the track was the length of the Polocrosse field.

Owners were to sit in the back of a pickup truck calling their dogs whilst a handler held them at the starting line until the starter gave the order.

On the morning of the race, Jimmy decided to be lame on his front leg much to my disappointment but rather than face the humiliation of withdrawing, I took Bondo my fox terrier who was also fast but not quite to Jimmy's speed.

The race commenced.

The third entrant took off in the opposite direction, Mary's hesitated and was not sure what to do while Bondo responded to my call and followed behind the truck and in the lead.

Mary's got the idea and chased after the truck and whilst approaching the finish line, the crowd cheered for their choice in a winner.

Bondo stopped in her tracks to see what the fuss was about and the skippy won the day.

I returned home to find Jimmy sound and well and sure he was playing truant.

I ran over Jimmy one very heavy rainy day. We were in the house when two bedraggled tobacco inspectors turned up at the front door saying their car had skidded off the road coming down the hill. "Could I tow them?"

I went to the sheds and brought out a four wheel drive tractor and whilst negotiating it past the barns to clear the spray booms attached to it, I noticed a splash in a pool of water as my front wheel was about to enter.

I turned the steering but was too late as

Jimmy came hurtling out howling. He loved water no matter if it was a brown muddy pool on the road.

I picked him up but could see no obvious injury and ran down to the house, called Sue to jump into the car and hold him whilst I drove him to Harare to the vet.

It was a VW Golf and we roared up the muddy road and past the tobacco guys waiting to be towed out. With no explanation, they must have thought me very rude.

Charlie Waghorn, the vet, took him in but he died sometime in the night. I was gutted.

My son Nicholas arrived five years after Tara and dare I say it, well planned. I wanted a son and got him. Unlike Tara, he was well trained; he slept at night and was not fascinated by what came from his nappy. He was an easy child.

Tara had a passion for horses.

I had my horse in the garden for some reason, probably going for a ride with her but she walked behind the horse unnoticed and got kicked.

In floods of tears, I picked her up thinking she had been injured but it was her pride that was hurt as she went off in a temper "why did he kick me? He is my friend!"

It was time to get her a pony of her own

and I had my eye on a beautiful grey Shetland that Mrs. Bishop of Karoi had bred.

Mrs. Bishop had taken weeks trying to encourage this little Tequila to enter the horsebox by bribing her with food but she would not enter.

Eventually Tara and I went up in the lorry to fetch her thinking it would not be a problem with a big open lorry. Wrong, she dug her heals in and would not leave home.

Now normally, with a difficult horse like that, I would rope her in, but Mrs. Bishop was fussing over her baby and her reasoning was not being heard by madam Tequila.

The cook arrived saying there was a phone call for the madam and off Mrs. Bishop went.

Here was my chance, ropes quickly attached and before Tequila knew what had hit her, she was in the truck.

Mrs. Bishop came back, "Oh" she exclaimed all surprised, "how did you get her on?" "Just walked in Mrs. Bishop, just walked in!"

Tequila was a fiery little thing and not really the right pony to instill confidence in an eight year old. But Tara impressed me.

One afternoon I was at the stables and heard galloping hooves coming down the driveway. It was Tara on a bolting Tequila and heading for the stables.

I did the dad panic trying to catch her as she

entered the stables. But Tara had hung on like a monkey and not at all fazed when I got her off.

Tara had a way with horses. I had some money in my account to go and buy eight Brahman bulls from Boss Lilford, who, as an eccentric character and extreme right wing politician was the master mind behind the Rhodesia Front party.

I selected the bulls and found I had some change, so knowing that he bred race horses, asked if he had any for sale.

He had and needed their stables "so buy all three" he says to me. One I didn't like, one I really liked and the third I was 'iffy'.

I took them around his race track and the one I liked was a Rolls Royce. 'Iffy' had attitude, wanted to eat you at the stables and to part company with you on the track.

Fortunately I was out of site around a gum plantation so we could settle our differences with a gum stick persuader.

I didn't have enough cash to buy the two at his price but made him an offer for the two. He rejected this but still complaining that he needed the stables.

I wrote out a cheque for the eight bulls and one horse, and then he has a second thought. "OK," he says "I need the stable, take the damn thing".

I wrote out a second cheque. It now came

down to loading.

I was not going to do two trips. My lorry could accommodate them all and that was that but Boss was not going to have it.

Nice and calmly I loaded the bulls and barricaded them in the front half of the truck.

Next it was the horses but Boss now interfered and created a big fuss that got the Bulls going crazy.

It came down to the battle of the wills and I was determined to have my way.

Magaba, my groom, was getting belted around the ear whilst he was told to pull on one end of the pole as Boss is pulling the other end of the same pole. It was a comical tug o war only Magaba was getting slapped for it.

Having secured them all in, an African, standing on the ramp watching this drama was asked by Boss what he wanted.

"I want a job!" he says. I couldn't believe my ears.

They all settled once we were on the road and got back to the farm safely. 'Iffy' was called Monsieur le Beau, Bowie to me and was an eight time winner on the track.

I warned Tara of his bad attitude and threatened her with a hiding if she goes anywhere near him.

My horses come in for lunch and on this

particular day I heard a little voice coming from the stables as I walked past from the barns.

I found Tara under Bowie's belly picking up the Lucerne that he was spilling and was feeding him and I watched dumb founded as Tara and Bowie had struck up a relationship.

That horse became calm tempered ever since then and became my top Polocrosse horse.

Tara was not competitive. We went to watch her sports day at Lilfordia Junior School, a quaint farm boarding school.

Lining up for a track race all the pupils readied themselves for the starters order but not my daughter. She was trying to establish the right pose for the camera and was still in that mode when the runners were well into the race.

Having snapped her out of it she sprinted to catch up with the back of the pack and proceeded to have a good chat. I felt like running on with a tea tray and scones to complete the picture.

She was like this in Polocrosse; a melee was an opportunity for a gossip. She has always been a people oriented person and will always go out of her way to chat to strangers.

Not to say she was not naive. As little kids Tara and Nick would wait for me to bath then jump in and take up all the space. I would cup my hands just under the water and invite them to see the frog through the gap between my thumbs, then squirt them. With Tara I could repeat it soon after and she would be none the wiser.

Nick went to Ruzawi Junior School in Marondera. When I took him he would cling to my legs, in floods of tears and beg me not to leave him there as if he was being sent to the slaughter house.

This did not do my emotions any good so I passed the dirty deed to his mom. They always seem so much better at it than dads.

I went to watch his very first swimming gala.

They had to swim the width at the shallow end in doggy paddle. On starters orders they all jumped in but Nick took forever to surface.

This did not auger well with me and I became anxious. Encouraged by the fact that the teacher was watching from the edge, I watched as Nick spent more time under water than on the top, each time he surfaced for air his puckered lips were stretching out like a submarines conning tower, and growing.

The kids were out of the pool when Nick reached the halfway mark and by now you could see he was tiring as he was spending more time at the bottom, but the teacher just looked on unconcerned.

I could not take any more of this. I was not

about to see my son drown and got up from my seat to do something about it. Richard Games, who was sitting next to me, grabbed my arm and said sit, it will be all right.

Nick finally made the end leaving a murky sand trail at the bottom of the pool behind him.

First to be seen were his fingers clawing at the edge of the pool, followed by extended lips sucking in all the oxygen his little body could take….and the crowd of parents rose as one and gave him a standing ovation.

Nick being the showman that he is, found enough energy to respond as if it had been his party trick.

Sue's younger sister, Judy was going through a bad patch. Doctors had diagnosed her as a chronic schizophrenic and they tried all sorts of different medications and counseling to stabilize her. Some of them, to me, appeared harsh and as she wasn't making much progress we discussed bringing her out to the farm in a more peaceful environment.

Judy's behavior was unpredictable and so she was heavily sedated.

Little Nicholas was trying to eat a wire garden table when Judy picked him up and left all his new teeth behind. It took well into his life to have them grow again.

There is a tree outside our bedroom

window and occasionally bush babies would come in the night, climb the tree and make such a racket that no sleep was possible. I would go out with a shotgun and chase them away.

On this particular occasion, running down the passage in the nude and armed with a shotgun, Judy decided to come out of her bedroom and watch the spectacle of me running around under the trees blasting away.

She was still there as I came back down the passage. "Good night" I said, "good night" she replied trying to comprehend what she had just witnessed.

Amongst the animals and the calm of nature, Judy was slowly coming right. She had been a highly respected nurse and when we felt she was over it, we discussed her going over to the UK to complete her midwifery nursing course.

I had some funds in the UK so it was easy enough to book her into college and pay for it.

Judy left on an open return ticket and she would write to us.

After some time the letters were sounding a little odd and raised alarm bells that we made enquiries.

Judy had not gone to college but instead had got back involved with the Rhema Church that I felt were the cause of her problems back home.

A London bus driver, I recall, had somehow

raised enough money to buy a fancy property with a double storied house in Exeter that he turned into a religious holiday retreat.

He 'employed' young girls like Judy as maids and their wages were board and lodging. They were made to hand over all their personal belongings including clothes, as an offering to god and given work suits in their place.

I rang this guy up on the phone. He told me Judy was becoming unstable and that he wanted to put her on the next flight home.

I told him not to do this and waste the ticket and that I was coming over to fetch her.

I arrived in Exeter to find Judy had been sent to the Exeter Mental Hospital and because she had slapped a nurse, had been put into a straight jacket and locked up in a padded cell.

I discovered that this retreat guy had gone ahead and booked her flight so now the ticket was useless. I also discovered that Judy had nothing except a shoebox of personal papers and letters. I had a very testing time with this opportunist.

Back at the hospital I spoke to her doctor, an Asian, who said they still didn't fully understand the disease and how to deal with it but that they had her under heavy sedation. "You have the best people to deal with this back in Zimbabwe" he said much to my surprise.

But Judy seemed reasonably together in my

time with her in those beautiful hospital gardens.

I went into town to do the most embarrassing thing any man has to do. Buy her clothes from her under ware to her shoes. The doctor gave me some emergency pills in case the high altitude got Judy going on the plane and we arrived back in Harare without incident. In fact Judy was good company.

Judy stayed with us on the farm and when she was right again she decided to move to Australia.

She fell in love with a man and married him and they went on to have two children, a girl and a boy.

But this is not the end of the story. Judy has raised and fostered somewhere in the region of forty children, many from babies.

Not only has she conquered her affliction but become a modern day saint.

In the meantime, back at Chiringi, I was still suffering from insomnia until that magic hour of 3oclock in the morning.

Sue would curl up in that foetal position of hers and once I sat on the end of the bed and sketched the scenery around me.

Sue with her hair in a birds nest with birds flying out of there and covering their ears from the sound of her snoring.

Jimmy and Bondo lying on the bed and looking at each other in disgust as Sue farted in synchronized harmony to that snoring, and me, sitting on the end of the bed yawning and looking forlorn with black rings around my eyes. Sue kept that drawing.

But William was always there at 5.30 with the tea tray and shaking my foot to wake me up.

Horseshoe was a fun community, Mary Leared would put on a Christmas pantomime and invariably I would be given a female role as with one of the ugly sisters.

And that would be right for me as I made a very ugly woman. We would put on three shows just before Christmas and would play to packed houses from around the community.

On one of these shows, Nicholas, sitting in the front with all the kids, recognized me and with a "That's my Dad!" proceeded to walk up on stage to join me.

There was nothing for it but to pick him up and continue the show without missing a beat.

Doing Father Christmas one year was a little unsettling for me as Nicholas bellowed and refused to entertain this weird looking creature despite the fact that this same creature, his dad, was offering him presents.

If you want to see what true love looks like, then see it through Father Christmas's eyes. The look of absolute adoration from these little faces is quite humbling.

I received a phone call one day from Mary's son, Harvey. He was putting on a beauty contest amongst all the young wives in the community.

The contestants would have to dress up for the occasion and walk down a cat walk in front of three local judges. The problem he felt, was that they would become shy on the night and asked if I would dress up in drag and lead the girls on. Secrecy was the issue.

I arrived at the club and joined my mates for a drink at the bar so that they could see I was there as one of the crowd. Of course the conversation was focused on who would be the winner amongst so many gorgeous females.

I slipped out of the bar unnoticed and Mary whisked me off to her house where I jumped into a bath and shaved my legs and removed my moustache.

Then Mary set too in trying to turn a toad into a princess with skilled make up procedures. The problem was shoes; no one had size 8 high heel shoes. Alison Wyrley Birch had big feet but didn't wear high heels so she was let in on the secret and I borrowed her sandals.

Arriving back at the club I was sneaked into

the kitchen to wait for the start of the contest.

In walks Edie Pearce asking Mary something and in mid speech stops and stares, very rudely I thought, with her mouth gaping wide open.

Quick thinking Mary now introduces me as a friend out from Harare to join the contest.

Trying to mimic a woman's voice was a tall order and I turned around to pretend to be cooking.

Time was up and as Harvey predicted, none of the girls would take the lead.

Coming through the bar from the kitchen, my way was blocked by a pack of men ogling at the women and the only way through to the front was to use my male muscles and barge my way through.

Talk of aggressive reaction suddenly turning to total disbelief.

I led the way onto the catwalk and proceeded to seduce the judges.

Mike was a judge and I targeted him but he kept looking away and became embarrassed that was unlike Mike. Wrongly thinking that my cover had been blown I thought Mike was being unsporting. Later he told me he had not seen such an ugly woman in his life before and could barely look at her.

He realized it was me when I left the ramp and he noticed the white farmers tan below my ankles caused from wearing Veldt Skoen shoes that were fashionable at the time.

Coming off the cat walk I approached Dave Smith whose wife was the winner. "Come out side with me Dave, and help me take my clothes off." I said wanting to prepare for my strip show next.

He backed off three paces, put his hands in the air in surrender and said "No way, I'm married".

If you think Father Christmas gets the best looks of devotion from adoring kids, try stripping and see the look of anticipation coming from the men. I have seen it all.

I did a strip on the stage once that was about a silhouette behind a sheet. I used condoms filled with water that gave the right shape, wobble and nipple as breasts.

The crowd was seated thinking a stripper had been hired from town. Seductive music played as I went through the motions of removing my clothes one by one and tossing them over the sheet into the audience.

Down to nothing but underpants, my boobs behaved beautifully, as with any perky young girl but as the dance progressed the weight of the water stretched the condoms until I ended up looking like anyone's granny.

I heard a voice that belonged to my wife. "I recognize that box of frogs, it's a man."

There was an Australian visitor sitting in the front of the hall. Now realizing it was a man, he lost all sense of humour.

Sitting at the club bar chatting to Nev, he revealed an embarrassing story that had happened to him.

He had recently acquired a pair of Turkeys which he wanted to breed from. Apparently Turkeys are not efficient in that department and so referring to his Gwebi College notes he read up on artificial insemination.

It required holding the Cock Turkey between your legs and collecting the sperm through masturbation. This he did during lunch time when everyone had gone off for lunch.

Sadly for Nev, the gardener returned for some reason and walking around the house caught Nev in the act. One Turkey Cock went flying as Nev groped for an explanation.

Polocrosse is a great family sport and we would always look forward to the next tournament.

The horses would go on the lorry and we as a family, would bundle ourselves into the car and head off to where ever it was around the country, pitch tent and have a great time amongst friends and around the camp fire.

Off to Umboe the one year, I was watching a game and sharing a hay bale with what I thought to be a very elegant and proper lady.

She was a stranger to me and I presumed she had come to watch a family member play. Out of the blue she emitted a very loud fart followed by an apology of "Cabbages" and proceeded to watch the game as though nothing had happened.

I looked at her in amazement, particularly that such a small body could accommodate so much gas but then looked around to confirm that it wasn't all in my imagination.

It wasn't. Everyone behind us was looking at each other in that "did that just happen" expression whilst at the same time trying to contain their giggles.

These things do happen at the most unusual places. I attended a funeral with a friend of mine, Sue Calase, whose mother had passed away.

We all sat in the quiet chapel and went through the usual service. Towards the end, a very elderly cannon, a long standing friend of the family and one that taught me religious studies at school, stood up and shuffled his way to the lectern with the aid of a nurse.

I do know that the elderly have difficulty in controlling their bowel movements and obviously applied here, for he spoke forth in that sermon fashion that was punctuated in different sentences by loud eruptions of flatulence.

He of course was unaware of the

entertainment he was providing but what a wonderful send off for a dear old lady.

CHAPTER THIRTEEN
TIMBER CONCESSION

I was approach by a tall and thin strange looking African who asked me if I wanted to cut timber in the Zambezi valley. I was aware of the Government's crazy scheme to resettle villagers in the fragile valley.

It was known as the mid Zambezi Resettlement Scheme and it involved resettling villagers from over populated areas around the country caused by the return of combatants after the war.

It was a real cosmopolitan group that settled there and resulted in village structures being broken down so that ultimately a number of them returned to where they came from.

Government pegged out patches of land on a grid square basis ignoring the fragility of the terrain and villagers cleared their patch by burning down standing trees.

Thousands of acres were going up in smoke driving the wild game away and being reduced at the hands of the poachers who used anything from .303 rifles to carbines firing bolts and cast iron pot legs.

I asked this man who he was. "I am the ward councilor for Masomo" he said "I know you well but you don't know me unless I tell you my 'chimerenga' name then you will know me well." [War name]. "Dust Bazooka is my name" he said as cold shivers ran down my back.

This man was the political commissar of our area and led an extremely aggressive group in the adjacent communal area. Here was this man in front of me who was responsible for the deaths of Arthur Beamish and my friend Ian Brown not to mention all the others.

He was the one who attacked me so often as well as my neighbours. "I could have killed you but I spared your life." He said unconvincingly. He then went on to tell me an incident that I remembered well.

At 3 o'clock in the afternoon, when all the workers had locked down, I decided to run up in the Land Rover and check a land at the top of the farm. Whilst there I decided to walk around a mountain, a short walk, to check on another land instead of driving all the way around.

Whilst in the tree line I heard a noise and dived for cover. I listened and looked but there was nothing I could see so I put it down to a wild animal, maybe a duiker.

But the sound was different, not like an animal and I retreated with long strides back to the Land Rover and drove straight home.

I had remembered that incident as clear as a bell and here he was providing the details. Why, when he had the opportunity to do so did he not take me out? Being charitable cannot be the answer. "We tried to kill each other but now we are doing business together" he said with a rare laugh.

I obtained a concession to recover the timber from both the Muzarabani District Council as well as the Guruwe District Council.

It took days of frustration and lengthy negotiations to settle on a royalty rate but I now had the concession that covered the whole of the mid Zambezi scheme.

I bought a frame saw in Chiredzi, the other end of the country with no idea how it worked and went down in my car with the lorry and trailer following on with Takesure and assistants to help dismantle it.

The machine was a huge solid cast iron Robinson, stood nearly two stories high, half of which was in the basement with the logs being fed into the top half that was at ground level.

Two five foot flywheels kept the frame of twelve blades in perpetual motion that rose and fell in an intimidating fashion.

It took us a week to dismantle this thing and with the use of a crane finally loaded the lorry and trailer.

I underestimated its weight and it took the poor over loaded lorry three days to reach the farm having gone through a number of burst tyres.

A crane was hired from Harare and the beast was settled in its new home on Chiringi.

I had taken the wise step to hire the operator for the machine and soon we had it fired up and cutting the first load of Mopani logs that had been delivered from the valley.

Mopani is a very dense indigenous tree that has the added problem of grit ingrained in the timber. It is a favorite meal for elephants that strip the bark and thus create an open wound for dust and sand to enter.

It is then ingrained into the wood as the tree heals and grows and on many occasions we would cut through .762 rounds from the war that had healed deep into the timber.

But setting up twelve blades with the right tensions and keeping them like that whilst cutting through timber it really wasn't designed to do, was a mission.

Blades would deviate from their line, visiting their neighbour on one side and then switch to visit the other that gave the impression of a bunch of stick drawings doing the waltz.

The frame saw was a big learning curve for me, teaching me that I was on the wrong track to commercially cut these hard indigenous timbers, so I decided to design and make a machine more suited to the timber and to alleviate the need to haul heavy logs up the steep escarpment.

My machine therefore had to be mobile and be able to cut at source.

The first attempt failed but through modifications, proved to be effective and so we moved into the valley and commenced cutting.

Two South African timber millers had heard of my unique machines and flew up to Mzarabani to see for themselves.

Unique in that at that time logs would be pushed through a static and large circular saw blade of usually over a meter in diameter.

To me that represented a large disc brake that required a huge amount of horse power to run it.

My machine had two small circular blades, an upper and a lower that followed the same cut line and allowed for far less horsepower. The whole unit traveled over a static log, requiring less track to clear the log.

These two South Africans watched the machine at work for quite some time before they uttered a word. "This machine shouldn't work" said one of them. "It goes against the principles of a static blade where it can be kept stable from all the energy forces it produces." They left scratching their heads.

But the next problem was Bazooka himself. He liked to be in control and would exercise this by stopping operations at the drop of a hat.

A meeting would be summoned in some remote area and we would all gather to find Bazooka absent.

He would be somewhere some distance away and I would send a driver in the Land Rover to fetch him, but he would refuse the lift and instead would insist on walking through the bush to get there.

A whole day would be lost and at times longer, before he was appeased enough for operations to continue.

Later, he upset the councils and must have done something wrong for the council at Guruve to have him locked up.

The project was bigger than me if I was to make a dent in the timber being destroyed from fire by the settlers so I approached my farmer friend Basty Rous if he would join me and invest into the project.

But despite the two of us putting all we had into it, it clearly needed the big money investors and Basty set it up.

They arrived at Mzarabani to see the project in operation.

I had built a tractor driven double bench saw that cleaned up the wane on the planks. We all gathered around watching this machine at work when I noticed the one operator flinch and stand back.

I looked to see what his problem was and fortunately I was close enough to him to notice a saw blade tooth hanging from his neck that had just penetrated the skin and hung there.

I quickly yanked it off and told him to shut down the machine on some pretense so that I could divert the crowd to another operation.

The culprit was a blade that uses inserted teeth and one came free from its holder. I have never used those blades again.

The investors came on board and money was made available to grow the company. They also invested in another chap in Harare to use the Marula timber we were cutting to make knock down furniture for the American market.

It was all go and I designed and made machines to suit our purpose.

I recruited staff, mechanics and mill operators and we set up a residential village on the banks of the Musengedzi River at a beautiful spot below the escarpment.

It was a lovely camp that we built under big shady fig and acacia trees and constructed cabins using timber off cuts and thatching grass for the roof that kept it very cool in the intense heat of the valley.

We lawned the area and kept it lush and green from water we pumped from the Musengezi.

In the evenings we would gather for a few beers and a sing along in the communal building that had a kitchen at the one end and bar at the other. I had a great bunch of guys predominately from the Beatrice, Featherston area.

The office block was on stilts designed around huge Baobab trees that one of them we built a shower in the hollow of the tree. Amongst the many offices was a clinic and I hired Brown to run it.

Brown had been a medic in the war but on the guerrilla side and I figured he must be good given that he had to deal with gunshot wounds in the middle of the bush and with very little to treat them with. He was good and a pleasant character with it.

The valley is a bad malaria area and we frequently got the disease in various severities. On one occasion I got it bad and became delirious. Brown suggested I be taken to Harare to hospital but I insisted he would do better and he did. He sat at my bedside throughout it all and pulled me through.

The valley was a tough place to operate. The heat was one thing. In October I would have to cut a candle to no longer than an inch in length otherwise it would droop in the evening heat, but the road conditions would test any vehicle working the corrugated roads.

I started with the old petrol 6 cylinder Land Cruiser but being hard sprung it rattled itself to pieces and often the engine would fall off its mountings and land on the front axle. The brake pipes would vibrate and break resulting in no brakes for most of the time.

On one occasion, going up the escarpment it boiled and lost most of its radiator water.

With no available water around we all took turns and pee'd into the radiator until it was full enough to proceed.

This truck was open, had no cab and the stench of boiled pee wafting back on us was unbelievable. There was nowhere one could put your head and gasp for fresh air.

We flushed it out several times but the stench remained for quite some time.

Gary McMaster was my workshop manager and

when he used this truck I advised him to run it into the embankment if ever the brakes fail going down the steep escarpment.

On this occasion he was travelling down with a couple of guys in the back and on approaching the first hair pin bend, he realized his brakes had failed.

As the speed at that point was not great he shouted to his guys to jump off. One did but the other was too scared and as he started to pick up momentum Gary shoved the nervous fellow off who somersaulted into the ditch.

Gary rode the roller coaster bends as the truck picked up speed for a few kilometers until he got to the bottom of an incline that led to the next set of down ward bends.

The truck slowed down on the uphill enough for Gary to jump out and pick up a rock to throw under the wheel but he couldn't keep up.

By the time the truck reached the crest Gary was able to catch up to it but by now it was starting to pick up on the downward momentum. He threw the rock under the wheel but the Land Cruiser ignored that and rode over it gathering speed as it did.

This time, without the burden of a rock Gary was able to catch up with a good sprint.

Managing to grab the back of the truck he climbed in with only time to lean over the seat and grab the steering wheel as he sped down the next set of hairpin bends.

Finally, on the next incline he was able to run it into a pile of gravel that a kind bulldozer had left for Gary's benefit.

I asked him why he didn't follow my instructions particularly right at the beginning when the truck speed was slow. "Because I would have had to fix the truck!" was his reply.

Sitting at a board meeting on Chiringi one day, we were told by a member of the board that he had approached the Vice President of Zimbabwe, Joshua Nkomo if he was prepared to invest funds from the Zimbabwe Development Trust Fund [ZDTF] and in effect replace the funds the investors had put in.

These members would then be risk free but still involved. That would put Basty and I at risk and I freaked realizing the implications of it all.

The investors also freaked as their huge investment would be at risk as soon as a government minister became involved and they were not to be trusted with any promise.

We all realized that as Vice President he could simply shut us down and take it over himself under the guise of the ZDTF. After all he had control of the concessions which, without it, we had no operation.

The ZDTF was Nkomo's brain child. He raised funds from external donors to purchase and fund ventures that would promote and benefit local peasants. The concept was a noble one but blinded by smoke screens.

As predicted he shut us down by cancelling the concessions and told us to remove our equipment.

He was bringing in new sawmilling machines from Finland and he would resume operations.

I knew the Finish Cara saw mill was not suitable for our dense hardwoods as it was designed for high production on softer timber like pine and so the project looked doomed from the start.

Victoria Chitepo the then minister of Natural Resources tried to intervene as there was no love lost between her and Inkomo but she was junior to him and was ineffective.

Likewise, the councils tried to hang on to their windfall in royalties knowing full well that that source would dry up.

I had piles of logs on road sides ready for collection but was not allowed to touch any of them and they were still there rotting away some twenty years later.

Nothing materialized from the ZDTF and all the timber in the scheme was destroyed through fire. We too had seriously burnt our fingers.

As a result the furniture factory collapsed and was put under the hammer.

CHAPTER FOURTEEN
CENTENERY. FEATHERSTON

With the collapse of the valley timber operation, I had no option but to sell Chiringi to clear debts and move into a rented property in Borrowdale, Harare. It was a lovely property that was big enough to keep my horses.

I put together some homemade mills and purchased eucalyptus trees in the Centenary area to mill into planks mainly for pallets and slat packs. It put food on the table and later I moved the operation to Featherstone.

But whilst at Centenary, a bush fire swept through the plantation resulting in a fireball of burning gases to land on the sawmill. I only managed to rescue one tractor, all the rest was burnt to cinders.

Whilst I was still operating in the valley, Bash Ibrahim, an Indian friend who ran a large transport company in Harare, wanted to invest 'in anything I chose to do'. He was keen to partner with me but I had resisted.

Now, a time in need, I approached him to join me in the Featherstone operation. He was happy to do so and in time we started a sister company to value add the timber into finished products mainly for the tobacco industry.

Through Bash I acquired an old Leyland AEC 30 tonne truck that had been rotting away at the back of his yard. Takesure and I stripped the thing down and rebuilt it.

I had received a timber order from the Cutty Sark Hotel in Kariba that was in the process of renovating and so decided to take this truck on a 'run in' trip.

I took Takesure, his assistant and the driver although I drove it myself. We got there without a hitch and off loaded.

On the return trip, a Zimbabwe Electricity Supply Authority [Zesa] technician was returning to Kariba in his Land Rover towing a caravan after a stint in the bush.

His clutch was slipping going up an incline between Kariba and Makuti and he attempted to turn the unit around just before a sharp and blind corner.

I happened to be coming around that corner when I saw my path totally blocked.

The technician and his assistants

disappeared down the slope as I ploughed into the caravan, a deliberate choice being the softer target.

Everything went dark as I wore the caravan like a glove and I forced the truck into the right hand embankment dragging the Land Rover as we went.

Takesure opened a hole for the driver and I to extricate ourselves out of the cab and a passerby went to alert the Police and to summon the Zesa crane.

The Police arrived in a clapped out Datsun pickup truck, took our statements and returned to Kariba.

I sent Takesure back with them to buy engine oil, plastic putty and a selection of bolts and tying wire, all that I felt I needed to get the truck working again. After climbing into the back of the Police vehicle they disappeared around the corner.

In the meantime the crane arrived and we used it to remove the caravan from the cab and as the front axle of the truck had been ripped off, we hoisted the front end and brought the truck to a clearing at the bottom of the hill.

Takesure returned with everything I needed but with a sullen face. "What's wrong with you?" I said. "I don't want to work for you, I am putting in my notice!" he mumbled over his shoulder.

He then proceeds to tell his sad story. Standing at the back of the truck and looking over the cab he realized a crash was imminent. He turned to warn his assistant dozing in the sun but no words would come out of his mouth. "That's the first time I nearly died" he complains.

He then climbs into the back of the police pick up and the police drive off at speed. Around a corner a warthog sprints across the road forcing the Police to take evasive action by driving into the culvert. "That was the second time I nearly died when that pig with its aerial pointing to heaven ran across the road."

They proceed until they come across an elephant in the middle of the road. The Police stop to wait for it to move off. "But that Nzou came walking towards us with its hand high in the air. I am sitting in the back of an open pick up and that Nzou is going to pick me with his hand and that is the third time I nearly die." "No, No, I don't want to work for you anymore."

We survey the damage and I tell Takesure that we will sort it out in the morning and in the meantime put my bed under that tree and let's get a fire going for sadza.

He looks at me in that disbelieving fashion and says horrified "Do you know there are Lions here! I refuse to make your bed there but I will do it in the back of the truck." Takesure ended up sleeping in the cab.

The next morning we set too repairing the truck. The radiator had a leak and the sump had a hole in it which we fixed with the plastic putty. The axle was returned to its place and fastened with the new bolts and the damaged fenders were tied on with wire as best we could. We arrived home without a hitch having been away for three days.

For a while things went reasonably well for the company. Saligna, a variety of eucalyptus was the commercial name used that also covered the Grandis variety of eucalyptus. At that time it had not been recognized as a furniture timber as it is now and our demand started to fall off.

Soon the company was getting into trouble and Bash suggested we go into bankruptcy. "You think that hand extended to you is there to pull you out of the quick sand" he says "It isn't, it is there to push you further in!" I didn't take his advice but hung in trying to revive it and pay off my creditors. It didn't work and eventually it came under the hammer.

Our marriage had been a rocky one and with all the stress it broke apart. Roger and Tara opted to stay with me and Nick left Ruzawi to join a very good junior school in Francistown in Botswana where

Sue eventually moved to.

Roger had just left Peterhouse Boys School and Tara was still at Peterhouse girls. Tara took on the new roll of being my 'mother' and with my sister Celia living in Harare, who has always been my 'mother', we got by.

If one has regrets in life it was not having the time in Nick's young life.

I took on a job with Jim Wilson. He had a sawmill in Norton and a single logging operation in Matabeleland run by a chap named Nolan.

The sawmill was not being fed adequate logs and Jim wanted me to beef it up and expand the operations.

I surveyed all the potential areas by vehicle first then took my horsebox with two horses to establish the potential of each forest for species.

It was fun and I was in my element. I would ride one horse and lead the other and after a picnic lunch would swap over.

I used to cover on average about seventy kilometers a day and arrive back where Custon my groom had set up camp and had the fire going. He was capable of driving the pickup and horsebox and would move camp daily as I progressed.

Some parts of the forest were fairly dense with thorn bushes and on one occasion, crouching carefully to ride through a thicket with my lead horse behind, the reigns got caught under my horse's tail.

He promptly clamped his tail, gripping the reigns like a vice and took fright as all three of us crashed through the thorns. I arrived back at camp with a torn shirt and sufficient blood to justify the event.

Yet again I was involved in lengthy Council meetings securing concessions all across the southern parts of the country, from Plumtree in the West to Mberengwa in the east.

I was not impressed with Nolan, a coloured man that had an enormous fuzzy hairstyle and icy blue eyes that he was quite scary to behold. The girls loved him though and he spent more time satisfying them than focusing on the other type of log.

I had to get rid of him if things were going to work and I had hoped he would make it easy for me by just resigning. He wouldn't so I decided to take him on my forest enumeration exercise and put him on a horse.

He was a tall thin chap and he had no idea how to ride a horse.

He would follow behind me complaining bitterly about his sore butt, aching back and rubbed legs and when I found an opportunity to trot, he would bounce about very precariously that I am surprised he still had his manhood.

Sometimes I would take a sharp corner or ride an obstacle and he would come bounding off in a pile of dust and complain that this was not in his job description guide.

On one occasion he sat in his crumpled heap and refused to remount. "OK" I said "I will see you back at camp but I must take the horse." We were miles into the bush with no human habitation anywhere and the thought of being alone did not impress him so he reluctantly mounted.

None of this did the trick and I ended up having to fire him.

With the increased logging operations I needed someone good to manage them.

He had to be that sort of person that loved the bush and was happy to be alone with no creature comforts.

I knew the right person, it was Mac Hill, an ex Selous Scout and a very good friend of mine. His company had also collapsed and was at a loose end so over a beer we discussed his prospects.

Mac is a split personality, on the one hand, as a past marketing director of Adam Bede, a furniture company; he was the true English gentleman with bowler hat and tails. On the other hand was a rough and ready bushman and he knew his bush. People who knew him as one, could never comprehend he was the other.

In a meeting with Jim, I told him of this new guy I had recruited. "Is this the Mac from Adam Bede?" he enquired "because if he is I cannot believe he is your man. Tell me this is not happening?" So I brought him around to meet Jim.

He arrived dressed in a sleeveless karki shirt, sawn off jean pants that were indecently short and tight and a pair of 'manyatella's' on his feet. [African sandals made from car tyres]. Jim is a lovely character and on seeing Mac, fell back in his chair and cracked up laughing. The anti thesis of the bowler hat and tails.

Mac settled into his new job like a duck to water. He had seen my camp and from then on we competed to produce the best camp using natural resources around us. It was great fun and the ingenuity that came out of it was stimulating.

He took me on Guinea Fowl shoots in his Hilux in which catapults were used. A rare head shot would result in a good pot roast that required two days of slow cooking. But always, around the campfire with several beers we would often yarn well into the early hours.

On one of these occasions I discussed my anxiety of Roger not holding down a job, some of them I had provided.

Mac considered himself a Psychologist and

so he asked me to employ him as his assistant "and I will sort him out, I need an assistant anyway!"

I read Roger the riot act and warned Mac that if he didn't pull his weight, I expect him to fire him. "If you don't, I will" I said with a serious air.

Mac wanted to use him as an enumerator to find productive belts of Mukwa and I asked that he search for new concession areas.

I sent down a horse for Roger to do it. Soon I was getting maps of beautifully coloured areas of different species that indicated rich pickings. I had been through these areas and must have missed it so decided to go down and see for myself.

I took Roger and Mac to identify these areas. Roger flounded, he had made it all up. Talking to the labour, I gathered that Roger would ride just out of camp, tie the horse to a tree and sketch fantasy maps.

Mac was embarrassed and I had to follow through on my threat. Fortunately, since then Roger has settled into a job that he has been in for quite some time albeit still having dreadful motor bike accidents.

I left Jim to join a partnership that the less said about it the better. It was a mistake to have left Jim and the partnership left me broken both financially and emotionally.

But I had built myself a double story tree

house in a magnificent Teak tree using off cuts from the sawmill.

Sleeping in a tent one night whilst I was building this house, an electrical thunder storm erupted. It was vicious and once it was over I looked out of my tent and saw an amazing spectacle that I have never seen since.

The ground was Kalahari sands and was shimmering in a glow all around the tree. The trunk at its base was likewise glowing. I used a torch to see if it was some type of glow worm but in the light the glow would disappear and I could not see anything in their millions that were responsible for this effect. With the light off it would return. They were microscopic and no one has produced a satisfactory answer to me.

Solomon, a barn boy I had employed at Chiringi joined me and his wife followed much to his annoyance. I gave her a job as my housekeeper as I still had Tara even though she was still at boarding school. I would look forward to her coming home at holidays and exeat weekends.

Solomon's wife was a challenge and a determined character with it. She had no skills, kept blowing into the charcoal iron that would send sparks flying to burn holes into our clothes and when she needed a rest, which was often, she would place the iron face down on the carpet making sure there was a fresh place to burn each time.

"Look at your wife!" I would complain to Solomon. "That is your fault" he mumbled "I didn't want her here and you gave her a job!"

Many years later Nick tells me he had fond memories of this place when he came to stay.

It was cold in that tree house in winter. The lounge was upstairs and cradled in amongst huge branches that some doubled as seats. We would sit in the sofa cuddled up with extra duvets and try and watch TV over the racket of a noisy generator down stairs with the cold coming up through the floor boards.

I heard a thump one evening and went onto the walkway that led to the lounge to investigate.

Sam, my Jack Russell liked that spot to take in the view that it gave and had fallen to the ground.

There he was fitting in the sand like a spastic. The first time I had had a Jack Russell that suffered fits and since then they all seem to have this distressing affliction.

At some time in the early hours, my horses in their paddock next to the house became panic stricken then settled down and stared in one direction. I could not see anything with a torch and eventually I went back to bed. In the morning I surveyed the area for indications of what it might have been.

A logging road went past the house and there as clear as daylight were the tracks of a lone

Elephant. Saddling up my horse I decided to follow this spoor to see where it had headed.

On the way I came across scuff marks in the sand that had continued for some distance down the road. Further on I found a very dead and squashed Monitor Lizard, just under a meter in length that had several puncture marks from being tusked by the elephant.

He must have been one very pissed off elephant to have brutalized this thing and to kick it so far down the road. I can only assume it had been wounded possibly by poachers and I was grateful he had not taken his revenge out on my horses.

He passed through my area and I heard no word of him.

I moved into a rented farm house in Nyamandlovu west of Bulawayo. I was in a precarious financial position after the partnership and I needed to do something but with no money to start anything.

Peter House School kindly gave me terms for Tara's school fees that bought me time, so I set out to design a mobile sawmill that could be towed by a light vehicle and operate in the field where the logs are.

There was a similar model available but mine had to have simplicity and be robust for African conditions.

So on my school drawing board I came up with working drawings to build it but I needed a sponsor to fund it.

I approached Ted Wilmot, a friend who had given me so much help and encouragement over that period and he put me onto an Indian owned engineering shop.

I cannot seem to remember his name, but he was enthusiastic and agreed to finance the prototype and to split the profits after costs on any sales thereafter.

I built the prototype in his workshops and took it on trials. After a few modifications we were ready to build a marketable one and demonstrate it on the upcoming Trade Fair.

The demo went well, cutting teak logs in front of respectable sized audiences.

It attracted the likes of the Forestry Commission and I was upbeat and out of that depressed state.

One chap says to me "It is all very well cutting planks, but let's see it cut the thinnest veneer and have the same dimensions from one end to the other"

"How thin do you want it?" I said confidently.

"Oh, make it 10mm" he said.

I set the machine to 5mm and took a veneer off the length of the log, handed it to him and gave him a tape measure. He was impressed and said "That is good, I am not a buyer but I am sure going to be your best advert."

Some hours later I was inundated with people that came from the pub saying there was a chap bragging about your machine and we want to see for ourselves.

I was running short of logs to demo but I could not resist this ego building opportunity and didn't mind wasting timber on people I knew were not buyers.

Some twenty years later I came across one of these machines cutting teak at Kenmuir on the Victoria Falls road.

As I only had my skills involved in these machines I had little control on the costs of production and as a result I made little from them but it helped to get me out of my predicament.

I had an important meeting to attend and I was anxious to impress two share holders of a company of my business proposition.

Sitting in their plush office I noticed an ashtray on the table and that they smoked so I asked if they would object if I had a cigarette.

Whilst engrossed in my sales pitch, there was a flash and a bang and tobacco flew in all directions across his table.

They stared at me in amazement as I said "What was that!"

"Your cigarette blew up and the filter is still between your lips." The one chap said as he started mopping up the table.

I was annoyed and had not seen the humour in it at all at the time and went home and reprimanded Nick as the guilty person.

He had doctored one cigarette with thin sticks of explosives and put it back in my box. I happened to pick that one at the meeting. It would have made an excellent candid camera shot.

CHAPTER FIFTEEN
SAFARI CRAFT

When I moved from Chiringi to Borrowdale I met Heather Walsh who lived not far from me and I kept her horse with mine. We would go on rides, play Polocrosse at Ruwa and became good friends.

When I was in Matebeleland she had very tragically lost her husband in a storm on Lake Manyami.

I felt the urge to return to familiar territory and I also knew in my inner self that I wanted to have Heather as my companion.

I still had no money but enough to make the break and Mike and Julie Cossey, long standing friends of mine, offered me a place to stay on their property.

It was whilst I was up there that Roger, who had a job in Bulawayo, had a terrible motorbike accident so Tara and I drove to Bulawayo through the night in my old Land Rover and in pouring rain.

He had been riding down the road opposite the Mater Dae hospital on his motor bike when a

Safari Hunter crossing the road connected him with the bull bars on his Toyota Land Cruiser.

The guy had his wife with him who was in labour and as with all us new fathers to be, he was in a panic to get her into hospital.

This knocked Roger and his bike into the path of an oncoming car that rode over him and dragged him, with the bike, underneath the car for about 100 meters before hitting a lamp post.

Sue drove through from Botswana and we met the next morning to see Roger in an awful mess. It was touch and go if he would survive but survive he did leaving facial and body scars that he bears today.

I spoke to Julie about starting up a venture in Harare. I felt I could start up something but I needed someone to watch my back and my finances.

My thought was along the lines of doing 'Fred Flintstone' style of chunky furniture and doing slat packs and pallets as bread and butter money.

"Yes" she said "I'll take the job" and as always, Julie was game for anything. But I was in no position to employ anyone and offered shares in this new venture.

I wanted Heather and Mike to join, but Heather was initially hesitant and Mike took several gin and cokes before he joined.

Heather made up some sample furniture using gum poles and faulted planks in her garage at home and whilst it was not what I had visualized, it was appealing.

Our lucky break came one morning when Elise Scheepers popped into the Cossey's and whilst in the kitchen was looking at my photo's of my tree house. "I want one" she says and I brushed it off as a usual comment.

Later that day she phoned and said she was serious. Kurt, her husband, was moving onto a farm that he was leasing and there was no accommodation available.

The farm owner had agreed to build a simple prefabricated house for them. "Can you do something within the same budget and the owner will agree. But I want a double story!" She pleaded persuasively.

I pulled out my school drawing board and designed a log cabin under thatch and Julie costed it. It could be done but with very little margin for us. Elise then suggested we use the finished product as a demonstration model to get new business and so Safari Craft was born.

The farm was beyond the Harare Airport and on this particular day I was travelling to site with Heather in her car.

I thought the time was right and suggested to her that I wanted a relationship with her. I should have done this closer to the site because she went into silent mode and left me squirming in the passenger seat for the rest of the way.

When she had given it lengthy thought, some weeks later I think, she accepted and I eventually moved out of the small cottage I had built on the Cossey's and moved into her Greystone Park house with her.

Tara and Roger continued to stay in the cottage as Tara had become Julie's assistant having now left school.

We finished the Scheepers house, messed up on the top floor boards and had to redo it so we came out with no profit.

But the house viewing day was well attended and launched us into something like fifteen years of building all around Zimbabwe.

We had a good team, Julie did the admin and finance, Heather oversaw the plumbing as she used to do that, and helped on costings whilst Mike ran the furniture factory.

A client would come to me with a vague idea of what they wanted. I was always amazed how so many people just cannot visualize in their minds eye what they want.

I would make a point of visiting their home to get an idea of their style, and then check the site out. Invariably the ground will tell you what fits. There will always be features such as view, trees, rock formations or simply the lay of the land, and it will always have its say.

Then I would sketch a floor plan and an idea of what the building would look like. At this point the customer would always say "Oh yes, know I can see it!" and make the adjustments they want. I would then do the working drawings and the girls cost it out.

We offered a turnkey product in that we provided everything including electrics and plumbing and sometimes landscaping.

We did not consider ourselves as builders but as creators of a product with the emphasis on rustic in all its scales of appeal. We built with stone, face brick and timber log cabin but always with a thatch roof.

It was very rewarding to design something and then go out and put it into reality and have a happy customer at the end of it.

We built all around the country, building homes, guest cottages, chalets overlooking dams and religious and recreation resorts.

It involved a lot of camping and I would take the boys, Heather's Ryan and Scott and my

Nick when he came up on holidays. They would take their pellet guns and the rule was 'shoot it you eat it'. So we had these grizzly things on the end of a stick and roasting over the campfire.

When I left Jim Wilson, Mac was moved into Mozambique to run a logging operation for Jim and whilst there, was casualty evacuated to hospital in Harare with an embolism.

He recovered but lost his memory and his self esteem. I brought him home to stay with us and as Heather was a nurse, was in good hands.

As his recovery improved I put him on one of our Harare construction sites, more to keep him interested and slowly his confidence returned.

A group of farmers were looking to move up to Zambia after the land invasions and were thinking of opening up a virgin block somewhere around Mkushi I believe and they approached Mac to recce the area to see what timber had value for milling.

Mac was excited about this prospect but I cautioned him not to do it. He was vulnerable to having a second embolism and I worried that the journey up and being in the bush would be very risky to his health especially as he would be on his own without assistance.

But Mac insisted. We gave him money and off he went in his car.

Some days later, Heather came into my office and said she had just received a phone call from Kariba asking for me and if she knew a Mac Hill.

"I am so sorry to tell you that your friend Mac has died." She said with tears welling up in her eyes. He had completed his mission in Zambia and was returning home and decided to stay over at the M.O.T.H. camp site in Kariba.

Typical of Mac, he befriended a fellow camper who invited him to go fishing with him the next morning.

At the end of the day they both went to the ablution block to shower and as Mac came out of the shower, this chap asked "Mac, are you ok, you look terribly pale?" With that Mac dropped down dead.

The friend went through Mac's wallet to find a contact number and found my business card.

Mac's body was detained in Kariba for some days for an autopsy before he was released but most of his valuables disappeared. He still had cash in his wallet according to his friend but that too disappeared.

CHAPTER SIXTEEN
INFLATION DAYS.

There had been a number of opposition parties opposing the government but one by one they were infiltrated and destroyed.

Morgan Tsvangirayi, a onetime union leader, formed the Movement for Democratic Change [MDC] and became the strongest opposition party to take on the government.

Commercial farmers, who employed a huge labour force, were seen on TV supporting the MDC with donations of money and some joined the party and stood for election to parliament.

Mugabe tried to push through a new constitution that would give him more powers and effectively secure him as the President for life but he underestimated the strength of this new opposition who successfully defeated the vote at a national referendum.

Mugabe was visibly shocked, followed by humiliation that turned to revenge. In 2001 he set his 'war vets' on the rampage to seize commercial farms.

With Army support and the Police instructed not to intervene, farmers were brutalized, murdered and chased off their properties leaving their worldly possessions behind to be ransacked and stolen.

Their labour suffered the same fate and a humanitarian problem arose with thousands of farm workers homeless and living on the sides of roads.

Squatters would settle on parcelled out pieces of land and looked to the government for inputs to crop it.

What once was the bread basket of Africa collapsed overnight to become a basket case of peasant settlers living from hand to mouth?

The economy collapsed, Industry took a hiding in its wake and inflation became rampant rising to three million percent after removing twelve zero's.

Food was scarce with supermarket shelves empty of groceries and with items such as firewood taking its place to fill up the shelves. Fuel became short and sold on the black market when it was available.

We lost our business in the rural farming areas but had rapid growth in Harare.

Farmers that didn't leave the country moved into the towns and cities where accommodation was needed.

We built cottages in the back of gardens, converted single storied houses to double story and extensions to existing buildings. We would run with eight jobs on at a time and with the inflation, would have to complete them as quickly as possible to prevent our profits from being eroded away.

The inflation was so rampant that we could not put an open ended inflation clause in our quotes as the client could only spend what he had.

A final quote would be upgraded prior to the signing of the contract where the client would pay a deposit of 50%.

This money would purchase all the materials required for the job and we would then rush to get the building to roof height where the client would pay a further 30% and then the final 20% on completion.

It worked well especially with our construction methods. We would roof over the existing house, propped up by gum poles and then remove the old roof leaving the ceiling intact.

The walls would then go up to secure the roof and the top story completed while the client lived down stairs.

That being done we then moved the client upstairs whilst we renovated the ground floor.

But then the problems started to set in as the economy collapsed further.

Fuel was a constant problem. Our vehicles would sit in the queue for as long as a week trying to get a small rationed amount and people would park their cars in queues that stretched around the block, jamming up traffic.

Some would take their scottle braai's and a good book to read, but for us, our lorries would have to collect our crews and drop them on site each day, make sure the crews received their materials and sitting idle in a queue was not going to do it.

Printed cash became the next problem. Banks would receive their notes in bricks and as inflation deteriorated, the bricks were never opened. You simply paid by the brick as against by the note. The printing presses couldn't keep up and note values were rising into the quadrillions.

Our clients would pay us by cheque; there was no other way to do it at that value. We would try to remove it from the bank before it devalued too much and spend it on materials but when the bank had no cash this money diminished rapidly in spending power. We could not issue cheques for our materials as they wanted cash and our sites began to starve.

When the note values got too high to

pronounce, the government removed a few zero's and the whole process would start again.

At one point, after removing the zero's they reintroduced the coins that had been laying around peoples cupboards. We went to the bank and joined the queue for our staff's weekly wages and filled up two big supermarket trolleys with bags of coins. But that didn't last long, inflation saw to that.

Not being able to finish the jobs on time was starting to cost us money and it didn't help even though some agreed to cover part of the inflation. We physically couldn't keep the sites going.

Some clients helped with fuel and accommodation for the teams and that helped us get those jobs out but we were crashing and I said to our directors, we clean up our jobs and get out before we go bankrupt.

While it lasted it was fun.

The building industry is required by law to shut down for a month over Christmas and as a family unit we would take holidays, usually at Mana Game Reserve, set up a lavish camp and have Christmas there.

On one occasion we had twenty two family members and friends and Heather and I catered for all of them having brought all our requirements down in the back of a lorry.

We had canoes on this trip in which we would start at Vundu point on the Zambezi River and row down to the camp at Nyamepi.

Friends of ours, Fannie and Kate Olivier had not done a canoe trip before and I persuaded them to come with me. Kate was very nervous and after some serious persuasion she relented.

I took the rear of the canoe whilst Fannie sat in the front and Kate in the middle and we set sail through the channels on the usual course that I was familiar with.

I was aware of a small pod of Hippo on a sharp bend in the channel and approaching this I advised Fannie that we must hug the left bank and skirt around them.

As we came into the bend, the current changed and pulled the nose of the canoe towards the Hippo. "Row to the left" I yelled, but all it did was make the canoe go faster towards the Hippo.

By now the Bull was alerted and came towards us threateningly. He stopped, you could see him think, 'this is not supposed to happen, they should be running away, scared!' then ducked as we skimmed over the top of him.

There was silence until around the corner "Fuck" Kate said with much feeling "I am never going in a canoe ever again!" It was a close call.

One year we went to Chizarira Game Reserve located south of the upper reaches of Lake Kariba.

The night before, I made my traditional Cornish Pasties ready for an early start to the long distant journey.

We set off in our convoy of Land Rovers, Heather and I in Queen Vic my 1957 series one and with every inch of space taken up.

Heather put the pasties on the floor next to her feet as space was limited and we would be eating them for lunch.

We all stopped at a lay by that commanded a magnificent view from the top of the escarpment and had these pasties for lunch. These pasties had been cooking in the heat from the exhaust pipe that comes through all Land Rover passenger floor boards but everyone enjoyed them.

It was a long tiresome journey on a corrugated and pot holed road before we arrived at the park.

Our camp site was quite a bit further on next to a river but we were advised that a flash flood had occurred and that we would not be able to reach it. We pressed on and decided to pitch camp near the river as it was now late and dark.

Dinner was the remainder of the pasties and everyone turned in exhausted.

Heather and I slept in the open and on top

of the Land Rover and it wasn't long before everyone, nearly simultaneously, was asking for the toilet paper and "Who's got the bodger badzer?"

The runs had started.

Little Kane, the youngest, called "Mum, I need a poo" followed by Scott and then Nick "Dad, I also have to go".

Heather, being a trained nurse now started to worry; toilet paper was beginning to run out so she rationed that, made everyone reuse their own private holes so that the rest of the country side was not planted with pasties and on return, made sure hands were washed with soap.

Nick, too afraid to venture too far, chose to do his behind the Cossey's tent in which, Kane I believe, took the blame for it. It was a good start to the holiday.

In the morning we discovered that the camp was just on the other side of the river and that the Parks information was wrong. There had been no rain let alone floods and the river was just sand.

We let the kids drive the Land Rovers across and settled into our correct camp.

My Land Rover rear diff packed up and had to be removed and for the rest of the time Queen Vic ran as a front wheel drive.

There were a couple of pools in the sand and one we used for bathing and the other for domestic use. It turned out a great holiday.

For a number of years we would form a team and join the Mana game count held every year in September and over a full moon weekend.

It was thoroughly enjoyable and involved about 56 teams walking in a line and spaced half a kilometer between teams.

A GPS or compass was needed to walk the three kilometers north to the shores of the Zambezi River, counting the number of game seen in their different species.

This would be done four times, once in the early morning and once in the late afternoon on both Saturday and Sunday and would give the organizers a fair average of game populations.

On arrival at Nyamepi camp, we would be briefed and co ordinates given. I was sitting in the front when the speaker realized he had been talking of GPS co ordinates and that there could be those with compasses. "Hands up those using a compass?" he enquired.

I put my hand up then looked around to find I was the only one. I had not progressed from my trusty army compass. None the less, I did keep a straight line and on a couple of occasions had the neighbouring team that used a GPS creep across into our transect.

On one afternoon walk, our way was blocked by a herd of cow Elephants with their young calves, walking across in front of us.

We stopped to let them pass but young Kane, Julie's son spotted a pride of Lion resting under a tree close to our left. It was obvious we could not wait there but our options were narrowed down by two Buffalo Bulls on our right. We managed to make a detour and completed our task.

The count has been going on for over twenty years and no serious incident has taken place over that time. Generally the game is used to people walking through the park and if one is sensible, is usually safe.

CHAPTER SEVENTEEN
MOZAMBIQUE.

Before we wound down the company, I was approached via someone to see Mick Clarke who was the project manager for the construction at the Archipelago Sun Resort in Vilanculo, Mozambique.

He was putting in six more chalets and wanted us to do the job but it had to go through the usual tender procedures.

I did the design of the structure so that it would withstand cyclone pressure and Nick made a scale model for me using plastic straws and I took the drawing and model around to Mick.

He was happy with it and Heather and I worked solidly for 36 hours doing the costing and completing a very complex tender document.

We won the tender but it came with a stiff two thousand dollar penalty for every day over the month that a chalet was not completed and with six chalets the project had to be completed within six months.

I designed it around panels of which the

main frames were double edged poles and set up a yard on Mike and Julie's property to treat and precut all the poles required and numbered them off ready for shipment. Each container had the exact poles for each chalet and so it was a simple matter to just erect them on site.

It all went well, two chalets were up and finished within the prescribed time but then the syndicate ran out of money.

Mike Cossey and I would alternate on a three weekly basis to oversee the job but now with the stoppage we had to stand down the crews of Mozambique workers that we had carefully selected and had molded into very good teams.

The penalty clause became defunct as instead of completing the project in six months it now took two years as money came in dribs and drabs.

Mick was good to us and gave us extra work that came up and we extended and refurbished the bar and restaurant but with all the down time made it difficult to hang onto our better workers who left to take up more permanent jobs.

There was a large Marula tree that grew near the embankment looking out to sea. From the old floor boards ripped out from one of our extra jobs, I built a platform amongst the big branches of this tree.

Every Friday evening we would gather for sundowners with friends and sub contractors and have a braai. It was great fun and I made a number of new friends there.

One evening, Ben, a youngster and scuba diver instructor challenged us old guys that he will fix us with 'Malawi Gold'. "Bring it on" I said always keen for a challenge.

He removed the tobacco from a standard cigarette and refilled it with crushed leaves of Marijuana and the three of us 'old boys' puffed away on it.

Initially I felt no effect, possibly from all the alcohol I had consumed but it snuck up on me and went directly to my knees.

I sat on a branch and said to my mates "How on earth do people win wars being supposedly psyched up on this stuff when I can't even stand?" This apparently was hilarious to all of us and the most stupid of comments would result in guffaws of laughter.

I was now bursting for a pee and I thought 'how on earth am I going to climb down this tree like this?' Just the simple thought of it I found hilarious.

Amazingly, by the end of the evening the effect had all gone and I was able to pack up and drive home. My first attempt at drugs.

In 2001, an opportunity arose to take over a small Dairy farm outside Harare for five years whilst the owners Alan and Marion Titterton went overseas to New Zealand to earn university fees for their daughter.

I leapt at the opportunity much preferring to be out of town. Ryan had just left school and I put him on there before we could move ourselves.

He would bring our milk into the office in town during the shortages days and we would have a queue of customers lining up outside the gate, some from as early as five in the morning, in the hope of getting a bottle of milk.

We could not meet the demand and I felt sad that we, as a country, had been reduced to this desperate way of life.

It was the height of the land invasions and whilst in Mozambique I decided to buy a piece of land on a river frontage outside Vilanculo to grow fresh vegetables for the lucrative market amongst the Islands and resorts.

It was my insurance policy if we got kicked off and we would have a ready business to continue with.

It started off with a lot of promise and I recruited a lady who was a great asset. She knew the game and set up the market but not long after, left to work for one of the resorts as they were able to provide her work permits where as I couldn't.

I built a cottage and pack shed and had the whole area under shade cloth and fully irrigated from the river. But I could not find anyone to run it that would stay.

I hired a single lady from Harare and took her down. I had heard that she was anti men so I stayed in the caravan and left her to free reign in the cottage.

Coming back from delivery she was in a huffy mood. "What's wrong?" I asked. "Oh those men of Vilanculo, they are so uncouth and whistling at me!" She protested.

I didn't think much of it but at around three in the morning I heard a car turn up followed by a lot of activity coming from the cottage. I put on a pair of shorts and went to investigate.

This dear lady was leaving and had organized a lift back to Harare. "Just like that!" I said feeling very miffed. I was due to go back myself having spent my time settling her in, now I had to phone Heather and tell her I was staying on to try and recruit someone new.

I failed dismally on that score;

Scott ran it for a while but moved into a profession that he is good at. Being a people's person he moved into the hospitality business and is doing well and is still there.

He was never a farmer but the knowledge

that it was a stepping stone to get him where he belonged, made me feel good.

I gave up after that and with the place being empty it got burnt to the ground when the security guard tried to burn out a snake.

I seem to be plagued by fires through my life.

Heather and I were in town in the Land Rover one afternoon when we received a call that the district was on fire from a bush fire that had started on a property downwind from us.

It was the 3rd of September 2007 and hot with a strong wind behind it. We were advised that our home was ok but that the fire was spreading out of control around us.

Heather phoned Ryan and asked him to pop across and check and we decided to return home immediately.

We knew that between the house and the road there was no grass to burn as it was our horse paddock and had been well grazed.

Ryan was back on the phone telling us a fireball of burning hay had flown right over this paddock from the neighbours hay stack and landed on the thatch roof of the guest cottage. Heathers parents were staying in that cottage having just arrived from Gweru.

From there it rapidly jumped to the storeroom Rondaval and then onto the main house that was a thatched double story.

We arrived when it had started burning the main house and I said to Heather "No heroics, it is only material stuff, we don't want to lose life."

Ryan had fortunately managed to get the gun cabinet out that had our private documents as well as a prized antique Burmese Teak elephant table that is a family heir loom.

Out of the blue, people turned up in their tens, grabbing whatever they could that had been rescued and left on the lawn and disappeared with it. It was a desperate situation that we could not control.

I had noticed that all the dogs were present and outside but at the end of it all we could not find Casper my Cocker Spaniel and presumed he was hiding somewhere in fright.

The next morning I found his charred body under my bed in the upstairs bedroom. He had run back into the fire and sought refuge under the bed.

Two fancy fire engines arrived from Harare and coupled up to the neighbour's large swimming pool to pump water onto the fire and despite emptying it we lost everything bar the clothes we stood in and some less important items that hadn't been stolen.

John Naested offered his cottage next door and we stayed there whilst we rebuilt everything.

Without us living on the farm, the theft

continued and I recruited the tenant living in the cottage on the farm, to oversee everything and hopefully minimize the theft, but it turned out that he was the biggest thief.

I said to Heather that come what may, we will move in by my birthday on the 18th of November and we achieved it on the 17th.

We were overwhelmed by the support given to us by neighbours and friends. From clothing to furniture we were looked after well, in fact, we ended up with more clothes than we originally had.

Dick and Sue Marr arrived from South Africa to visit and have lunch with us on the next day and as I had no way of contacting them to cancel, they arrived to find another disaster that they seem to find me in.

"Pocock, what is it with you that we seem to find you in some sort of problem?" Dick said with a loud laugh. He gave me 500 rand that he had on him and said put it towards the building costs.

Today that is worth US$50 but with the exchange rate at the time of the inflation; I was able to exchange it and had sufficient funds to glaze the whole house. Something that could never be done today in our US based currency.

Soon after moving onto the Arcturus farm, we met Bill and Fiona Clark who would pop in to buy milk.

I invited them to sundowners on the

veranda and as I was keen to meet all the small holders around me, we discussed having a regular Friday sundowner session as a wind down from the week.

It took off and is still going to this day since my five years on the farm has led to indefinite. But Heather decided we were not to drink on an empty stomach and so she made soup in a three legged cauldron. Since then the gathering has become known as soup kitchen.

Many wonderful friends have passed through soup kitchen over the years and despite the fire, it continued whilst we stayed at the cottage next door.

With the activities of the land invasions, everyone was tense and nasty political incidents would happen.

My head dairyman was discovered to be involved in milk theft with a particularly nasty war vet that lived in the adjacent reserve. He was fired and I banned the war vet from entering the farm.

He took exception and turned up outside my workshop with a load of tomatoes in the back of his Nissan Champ and proceeded to offer them for sale to my workers.

I told him to leave, whereupon he picked up a stick and threatened me with it. I looked around for the nearest thing handy which happened to be a length of steel water pipe and said "Bring it on, you want to fight I am also a war vet, come on!"

Sizing up my weapon he had second thoughts "Fuck off to British" he tells me.

"Fuck off to Zambia" I replied.

"I am not from Zambia" he says indignantly

"And I am not from British" I replied with emphasis.

Some months later I saw him talking to Heather at the garden gate and rushed up to tell him to get off the property. "He wants to borrow money" Heather tells me. I sent him packing.

Years later he was apprehended by a policeman for something that he had done.

The policeman jumped into his car and told him to drive to the Goromonzi Police Station, but instead drove home and promptly beat up the police officer.

Goromonzi Police retaliated in numbers and educated him with a good hiding, but I have never seen or heard from him to this day and wonder if he hasn't departed from this world.

Election time was always interesting. The ruling party would hire young thugs who would go around beating and intimidating people to vote for them.

One day they turned up on the farm and had all my workers sitting in a circle on the floor.

I was summoned and made to sit on the

side whilst they belittled me in front of my workers. Every time you said something you would have to say the party war cry with your right fist in the air.

Eventually my dog came to have a fuss made of him now that he had found me sitting on the floor. "You treat your dogs better than your workers! We will take your farm and we will beat you!" they emphasized pointing their sticks.

Sometime after the elections a couple of these guys turned up in a very different and submissive mood asking for a job.

"I can't employ you, you work for the party and remember, you wanted to beat me" I said

"Ah no, we were told we would get paid for beating people but now they don't want to pay us."

Ryan had taken the farm truck into town to collect a load of masese for the cows. His grandfather had gone with him and returning home, he was stopped at a police road block.

Unfortunately, Ryan had found an empty .762 cartridge case in the paddock that had clearly come from the war era.

This was now lying on the seat in the truck and this brought alarm bells to the police and they arrested him. Granddad was told to take the truck home.

I went around to the Mabvuku Police Station and found Ryan handcuffed in the back of a

Land Rover. The member in charge tells me he is taking him to CIO at Police Central in Harare.

From my experience before, I know that these young guys of military age can disappear amongst the police stations around the place, so I followed the Land Rover to Central and saw him being put in a cell in the dungeons.

I went upstairs and sought out a senior CIO officer but no logic would work here. They had their spy and enemy of the state.

I then resorted to the reality of the times, that of food as it was short. "Release him into my custody until the court date and I will give you 50kgs of chickens". This was tempting and it took a couple of more hours of the Friday afternoon for him to accept.

I took Ryan home and the next morning sneaked the chickens into his car at the back of the car park.

Monday we turned up at the Rotten Row Magistrates Court where Ryan was immediately arrested and sent down to the cellar to be with the other prisoners. He would be beaten as well.

In court the prosecutor presented the evidence and held it up. "Is that the cartridge shell that was in your possession?" the magistrate asks. "No" says Ryan "That is a .303 and mine was a .762" I cringed willing Ryan not to say too much.

He was given a fine and I went and payed it

but I was now more concerned about a police record that he will now have.

We had to go back to the police station to sign off and I persuaded the policeman to return with me in my Land Rover.

He agreed and as he had the court papers on him, I started negotiating a price in meat for him to burn those papers.

We settled on a few chickens and in the middle of Harare we burnt those papers on the Land Rover floor.

CHAPTER EIGHTEEN
THE FINALE

Recently, I took a trip to Lusaka, Zambia to visit friends and as I am on my own, decided to take the coach.

The fare was very cheap, less than a single police fine, and the journey, if one selects the right seat, was pleasant enough.

A Zimbabwean band was playing on the TV screen and one particular song had a good beat to it, so I said to the madzimai next to me "This is good music, do you want to dance?"

She cracked up in a laugh that had her expansive mass wobbling like jelly and then proceeded to tell the rest of the coach what I had said. In an instant all the passengers on board were laughing and clapping suggesting I do just that, 'get up and dance' they shouted in unison.

I declined and buried myself deeper into my chair.

The point of this story is that despite the hardships Zimbabweans face, no jobs, no money, a very weak economy and living in a police state, there is still humour amongst all this adversity.

Zimbabweans have always been able to laugh at themselves no matter the situation and by and large they are hospitable to their fellow man kind.

It is only the politicians who contaminate them through divide and rule tactics and generally it is the youth that are targeted as the easier to indoctrinate.

I once believed that my own generation must die out before all this racial antagonism dissipates but with the politicians targeting the youth, I figured that it would be perpetuated.

Generally one does not find racism amongst the ordinary adult Zimbabweans but you do see it in the youth and as young as junior school age.

The party politics had broken down village structures where the youth no longer respect their elders and this stemmed from the war era where the youth were given powers over their elders by forming them into spies known as Mujibas.

But I now realize that as the youth mature into adulthood and start living in the real world of hardships, their attitude changes and racism becomes less prevalent.

Now, there is a word in Shona that

particularly the youth use whenever a white person passes by and that, with the emphasis put behind it, I find derogatory.

It is 'murewa'. "Hey murewa" they shout as if we are some kind of alien. Apparently, the meaning behind the word is the odd one out in a troop of baboons.

The other day, driving through Epworth with my sun glasses on, one youngster shouted "Hey China", not referring to me as a friend but as a mistaken identity that I was Chinese.

With the Chinese becoming the new economic colonizers in Zimbabwe, will they become the new murewa's?

But despite all this, I feel optimistic that with the general good will of the people, there is hope for Zimbabwe and that it simply means that all that needs to change is the mindset of the politicians for change to happen.

Despite the fact the politicians are so well entrenched and difficult to change, Zimbabwe, yet again, can still be a great nation.

There is Humour in Adversity

FROM THE SAME AUTHOR

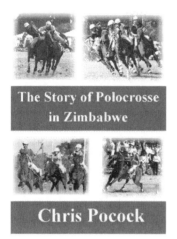

'The Story of Polocrosse in Zimbabwe'

Chris Pocock

With a foreword by Barry Burbidge past President, Polocrosse Association of Zimbabwe.

The book is an insight into the life of Polocrosse from its early beginnings in 1948 at Fort Victoria and covers 60 years of development through turbulent times to be one of the leading nations in the sport. It recollects all the characters that played their part through different clubs and brings out the humour, frustrations and determination that made this small turbulent country a nation to be reckoned with.

It digs deep into the past in search of where it all began before Australia gave the modern sport its name and follows through with the sequence of nations joining the global family of Polocrosse.

An easy read and with a lot of photo's, it takes the older generation down memory lane whilst giving the younger, a sense of belonging and a proud contributor of a growing sport.

The book can be bought online through Amazon.com in print and e-Book formats. Follow the link . CreateSpace eStore:

https://www.createspace.com/4146568

For further enquiries mail chris.pocock2009@gmail.com

Printed by Amazon Italia Logistica S.r.l.
Torrazza Piemonte (TO), Italy

17033576R00124